living IN THE *flow*

living IN THE *flow*

forty days *to a* supernatural faith *and an* overcoming spirit

DR. PAUL L. ALLYN

Printed in the United States of America

Packaged by Pleasant Word, a division of WinePress Publishing, PO Box 428, Enumclaw, WA 98022. The views expressed or implied in this work do not necessarily reflect those of Pleasant Word, a division of WinePress Publishing. Ultimate design, content, and editorial accuracy of this work are the responsibilities of the author.

Unless otherwise noted, all Scriptures are taken from the Holy Bible, New International Version, Copyright © 1973, 1978, 1984 by the International Bible Society. Used by permission of Zondervan Publishing House. The "NIV" and "New International Version" trademarks are registered in the United States Patent and Trademark Office by International Bible Society.

Scripture references marked KJV are taken from the King James Version of the Bible.

ISBN 1-4141-0309-3
Library of Congress Catalog Card Number: 2004097739

Dedication

This book is dedicated to my wonderful family whose love and support have been the backbone of my inspiration. I also dedicate this book to all believers who are about to discover the incredible beauty of life lived in the flow.

Table of Contents

Acknowledgements

How does one go about thanking all of the people who have helped you persevere to the end of that process called "writing a book"? First and foremost, without the constant encouragement of my wife, Eileen, this work would never have been finished. She never tired of nudging me ever onward and upward.

Special thanks goes to all of those individuals—pastors, mentors, and friends—whom God put in my life to give encouragement and direction along the way. Among them I would like to mention the following people: Dr. and Mrs. Daryl Merrill, Sr., Rev. and Mrs. Jack Wolf, Rev. and Mrs. Ralph Diehl, Dr. John Lloyd, Dr. David Shibley, Dr. Jeanne Moldenhauer, Mr. and Mrs. Ed Oleksy, and Rev. and Mrs. Delbert Wells. Their examples serve to remind me to always strive for excellence in the pursuit of God's dreams.

As anyone who has ever tackled the task of writing will tell you, writing without review is either foolish or evidence of a genius that I don't claim to possess. With that in mind, let me express my heartfelt thanks to a few members of our ministry team who were especially helpful in that department. Sandra Perdomo spent countless hours reviewing what I had written. Her invaluable suggestions helped make the book what it is today. Pam Mithum is deserving of thanks for having invested her valuable time and expertise in English literature to read the manuscript and for making many very welcome constructive comments that have immeasurably improved the finished product.

Above all, I thank my Heavenly Father who has been the inspiration behind it all. He taught me the lessons I have strived to share in these pages. Without His patient dealings with me, I would never have learned how to *live in the flow*.

May He use the words on these pages to help others do the same.

Preface

If there is one reason why the modern-day believer, especially in western countries where a "science and technology" approach to life seems to dominate the scene, often fails to develop miracle-working faith, it is found in an anemic spiritual life. The cause of that can be laid quite squarely at the feet of a pallid devotional life and the lack of personal, spiritual intimacy with the living Christ that such a state of affairs produces.

On the one hand, our culture forces upon us a sense-oriented and sense-indulgent type of life-style that works to inoculate us against the realms of faith. On the other, evidence abounds that God is, in fact, hard at work breathing into our souls the desire to reach out for more, to believe in the undeniable realities of the invisible, and to receive the impossible. If we yield to God, give in to this thirst for more, we will discover why millions around the world are waking up to a brand-new beginning in their Christian lives, why they would prefer those lives to any other and why, for them, there is no price too great to pay for the privilege of walking, one with Him, on the pathway of the Kingdom.

For spiritual power, miracle-working faith, and death-defying love to flourish, more is required than a courteous nod. After all, we are not talking about choices on a menu or preferences for this year's vacation spot. On the contrary, we are talking about the stuff of which spiritual adventures and godly greatness are made. To obtain this, it will be worth the effort, no matter what it takes. How is your *daily pursuit of God?*

While you ponder how to respond to that question, it might be helpful to gauge where you are in relation to the following spiritual mile-markers. For starters, consider the depth of your relationship with the Lord. We can always go deeper, but this must be done *intentionally*. In a day and age where terrorism threatens global stability and personal tranquility, at a time when we have seen towers of steel turn into heaps of rubble, at a time when more threats of the same are made, we need to tap into a source of strength and forward-looking hope that *cannot* be destroyed. We need a *flow of life* within that enables us to walk securely upon the waters of adversity. God is that source. The more we do to develop our relationship with Him, the more His strength and purpose will fill our daily lives.

Perhaps you are one of many who have used the over-worked excuse, "I have too little time." Excuses have never helped us very much or led to great discoveries. Excuses do not lead to empowerment nor cause us to overcome, but *truth-encounters* do. We would be better off to simply be more honest and confess, "I'm not interested." Or, maybe, just maybe, you are a card carrying member of that group that simply doesn't know how to get started. If that's the case, it really isn't so difficult to understand. Except for a thin veneer of pseudo-spirituality, our modern culture is nearly devoid of interest in true spiritual pursuits. Our culture has tried to take God out of the equation only to find that the solutions sought are only produced when He is put back in.

How do you know if you have let Him slip out of the top spot in your life? If you think the acquisition of all things material is vastly more important than certain intangibles such as a deeper walk with God, a greater hunger and thirst for Jesus, or the release of your faith to believe God for the miraculous in your life, then you have! If you just read the last few lines and quipped, "Oh, how quaint!" then you have. If your quest for the basics of life has become so stressful and all-consuming that you no longer believe that you have the time to pray or, worse yet, no longer care about it, then you have!

Most of us would admit that we make room for those things that are important to us even when we must make sacrifices along the way. It's time to discard the faded picture of God most of us carry around and replace it with a revolutionary revelation of who He is and what His kingdom is all about. If you accept this challenge to learn the *ways* of those who know the secrets of walking upon the water and living in its flow, you stand to be amazed. Forty days is all it takes.

I have seen it in my life. Without fail, God has more than met my expectations of Him when I have made it a point to seek His face in a special way. My wife and I have experienced the unbelievable changes such periods of pursuit are capable of producing. Sprinkled liberally throughout our lives, such periods open up wonderful new spiritual vistas before us. Such times, be they a week or even forty days, are often what is required to jump start our own, *personal* renewal and rescue it from the tangled mangrove of competing loyalties and limited personal resources. Through persistent digging, like the prospector hot after a vein of gold, or like the bloodhound relentlessly pursuing its prey, during such times, we break through the outer layers of frustration, hopelessness, and just plain weariness and release the vast flow of God's living water so that it can course unfettered through our being.

Introduction

Study the Scriptures and you will quickly learn that the people of the Bible whom God used to change history have been people who hungered and thirsted for God. The same is true of those He has used down through the centuries. They have not been perfect people any more than you or I are perfect, but they did share this in common: They sought Him with their whole hearts, forsaking all for the privilege of knowing Him and for the pleasure of doing His will. Foibles and failures alike did not stop these individuals. They pressed on in spite of them and learned to overcome. These souls sought God *long and hard*. They fasted, they prayed, they pushed forward, and they did their best to obey Him. God especially prepared them. He, as the Master Potter, shaped them to be the *deliverers of destiny* that shaped the history that gave birth to the world in which you and I now live. Aren't you tired of lifeless religion? Don't you wish God would use you in an extraordinary way? Doesn't your heart burn at the thought of it?

Look at the people God is using today and then answer the question. You could be one of them. Imitate *their* faith. Do what *they* have done. Learn from the great men and women whose lives *today* are leaving behind a proven track record of brokenness and blessing, obedience and fruitfulness. We are talking about individuals who have been, on numerous occasions, called to fast, pray, push, and then keep going. They were willing to deny the demands of the flesh in order to dig deeper in God.

How long, how much, and how hard is enough? It depends on you and God and what needs to be done. For some, it takes a day; others may take as many as forty days. It is my belief that while we must give wide birth to individual convictions as to length of time, we do not need to do so with regard to whether or not to seek God in this way. It is not a matter of if, but when. It is the way of the cross that leads to the crown and not the other way around.

I have designed this book as your guide on a forty day journey to a stronger faith and a renewed spirit. Why forty? Because whatever you manage to do for a period of forty days becomes an integral part of your life. It's no accident that the pattern of forty days is found throughout Scripture. The forty day miracle! This is true whether it's a new exercise program or a new spiritual discipline. Do it for forty days, and it's yours! Do it for forty days, and you are His!

These daily readings will serve to keep you focused on Him and finely attuned to His voice. They will teach you to navigate your way through difficult times into an ever expanding experience of His Person. Follow them, and before your forty days are up you will be flowing in the river of His purposes and plans.

This is how it works. You will need to read each day's selection prayerfully and then grapple honestly with the questions you find at the end of each reading under the heading "Pinpointing your location." The questions will help you take inventory of yourself spiritually, a very important step to activating miracle-working faith and bringing personal renewal. Honesty permits God's Word to do His work—hindrance free. It's time to break your addiction to dishonesty and doubt.

Next, under the heading, "Plotting your course," you are given a key thought that sums up one main truth expounded upon in the day's selection. Each thought expresses a spiritual principle which, if applied in your life, will keep you moving forward in your own personal revival. Just as importantly, it will put within your grasp the spiritual resources needed to successfully handle life's many challenges that pop up along the way.

Finally, the "Praying in your destination" heading gives you, the reader, the opportunity to meet with the Lord one-on-one in prayer so that you might ask Him to help you fulfill your destiny. The act of writing down what you are asking God for will help you avoid the common error of being so general in prayer that you don't know what it is you have asked for when you finished. The more concrete and specific you are, the greater will be the release of faith for what you have asked.

There is something else we should bear in mind as we begin this journey; we move together. Remember that from the beginning the Father's desire has been for all of us, not just one of us, to fully participate in His kingdom and manifest His divine nature. His great and wonderful promises (2 Peter 1:4) are available to each one of His sons and daughters. Yet He wants all of us to learn to corporately activate and release the flow of His divine nature in us. Nothing less will do! As we move together into the flow of His presence, incredible faith will grip us and propel us rapidly forward in the waters of opportunity into the wonderful future that is waiting for us.

For this to happen, we must move at His pace. Our journey into the presence of God is not a race to hurry up and win, but rather an experience to sip and savor. We move at a pace set by the depth and the intensity of our desire for more of God. It is extremely important that we settle in our minds early in our journey that it isn't the "distance" we travel each day that matters as much as the "depth" we achieve. If we determine from the beginning not to be in a hurry, then we will stop marking time like the market driven, modern individuals we have been, and see all around us, and begin to make Him the number one priority in our lives.

With these insights in place, you will be able to accomplish the impossible for God. You will meet each spiritual challenge with supernatural confidence. All of us who take this journey discover that God is not only with us, but in us. God Himself travels with us. He will be there to assist and help you to make the most of the awesome opportunities you will encounter along the way. Everything you learn on this exciting journey will equip you with the essential truths and insights that every traveler needs in order to face each day with the courage of a hero and the faith of an over-comer.

Many of us have discovered these keys and have begun to use them. What we learn on this road helps us on the next. As you do the same, the Holy Spirit will see to it that your journey takes you into the greatest personal revival of your life.

The days in which we live are days of great spiritual change. Spiritual revival is sweeping across the earth and impacting entire nations, preparing the way for Christ's return. *Our journey is best understood against this backdrop and our participation in it will prove to be more wonderful than we had ever imagined.*

. . . Beginning the Journey

Know Your Guide

"By day the LORD went ahead of them in a pillar of cloud to guide them on their way and by night in a pillar of fire to give them light, so that they could travel by day or night. Neither the pillar of cloud by day nor the pillar of fire by night left its place in front of the people."
(Exodus 13:21–22)

On every journey, you need a guide. Take my word for it, guides are important. A few years ago, I spent several weeks ministering in Indian villages up and down the vast and mighty Amazon River. The first time out on the river we got off to a late start which meant we would arrive at our destination after nightfall—a definite "no-no" for travel on the Amazon. It was not a pleasant prospect, especially since we were traveling in a small launch powered by a not-so-new outboard motor. Navigation by night on such a treacherous river was an invitation for disaster.

My first day on the river taught me respect for *this* living creature. Between the ominous whirlpools we had to carefully skirt and the huge trees the river hurled downstream like projectile missiles aimed at unsuspecting boats, I learned that you don't venture out on that river without a guide. Not just any guide will do either. You need a trustworthy one with knowledge and experience. My first night on the river taught me that you don't travel without prayer. When night fell, we were still on the river. We found ourselves in the middle of the fiercest electrical, wind, and rain storm I've ever been in. It is one thing to be safe inside a dry house far from the raging waters. It is quite another to be on an angry river when its defiant waters threaten you and those around you. We couldn't see anything except the glowing eyes of crocodiles along the banks and whatever other shapes our guide's flashlight could make out off the bow of our tiny boat. The rain pelted our faces and drenched our bodies. Finally, after several hours, we reached the mouth of the tributary that would take us to our destination.

The relief I felt at getting off the Amazon River itself made me forget all about having become a human sponge, dripping wet and tired. As though the storm were oblivious to our situation, it continued unabated. Somehow, I felt more secure on the smaller river even though it could be just as treacherous. My feeling of security was raised a couple of more notches when we picked up the two native guides who were responsible for taking us to their village some distance upstream around countless snake-like bends and turns. Frequent flashes of lightning silhouetted their forms against the night sky while they stood resolutely on the bow of the boat directing us first to the right and then to the left to avoid hitting submerged tree trunks and keep us from running aground on seemingly invisible sandbars.

An hour or so later we arrived. Time passed imperceptibly. We were all mesmerized by the hanging vines, the canopy of leaves overhead, and the constant lapping of water against the sides of the boat. The rain stopped and an unearthly stillness filled the night air. Without warning, our guides announced that we had arrived at our destination, the small Brazilian, Ticuna Indian village of Bon Pastor (Good Shepherd). Each member of the team was eager to get ashore. It didn't seem to matter that we hadn't yet reacquired our land legs. It was a short walk over the packed mud banks to the huts where we would sleep. All we could think about was setting up camp. We couldn't get our hammocks and mosquito nets up fast enough. The next several days would be very full, and we were going to need all the sleep we could get.

In spite of our exhaustion, we were exhilarated that our journey had begun. Once our guides saw that we were safely tucked away for the night, they disappeared into the night. Soon the stars began to poke through the now-parting clouds and the stillness of the jungle was interrupted only by the syncopated sounds of unconscious travelers snoring unashamedly, dreaming of adventures yet to come.

The team members were thankful that the Holy Spirit had been with them, His cloud by day and pillar of fire by night. His hand had led us into His safe harbor. Indeed, it's good to know your guide.

Pinpointing your location:

By what do you guide your life; the stars, tea leaves, or God's Word and Spirit?

Plotting your course:

Trust the Holy Spirit to guide you every day in the decisions you must make and you will fulfill God's will for your life regardless of the dangers you encounter along the way.

Praying in your destination:

1. ____

2. ____

3. ____

Get Off the Sidelines

"... and then he led me through the water. ..."
(Ezekiel 47:3)

Ezekiel writes of a river, a unique river that flows out from God to us. It represents His presence and flows from His throne to a world whose greatest need is for His presence. That is why deep within we feel the stirring of fresh spiritual desire. He is so desirous of our fellowship that He won't let us rest until He sees that we are taking steps to satisfy our God-given thirst for more of Him.

Who among us in not tired of sitting on the sidelines? The days are past when we could be content only to be spectators of the mighty works of the Holy Spirit. We feel sick inside when we contemplate the possibility that God might pass us by because of our reluctance to let Him reign as Lord in our lives. Our passion for Him, however, will not permit us to live so far below His high call. His *will* becomes our desire; His purposes become our destiny. Do you not see it? He is in the waters! That is where the miracle is. If we don't get in, we will miss the whole dimension of the miraculous.

Not long ago I received a vision from God. It concerned a high-ranking government leader whose life was in danger. As visions often do, coming and going in a matter of seconds, this one was brief—but very clear. I saw this leader at an outdoor political rally. He was face-up on the ground with sleeves rolled up, and his white shirt was stained in blood. The inference was unmistakably clear. He was dead; his life taken by an assassin's bullet. A young woman dressed in a bright red dress stood beside him. She appeared to be in anguish as she looked toward heaven, as if asking why. I knew what the vision meant and I knew I had to do something and fast.

Somehow I had to find a way to personally deliver the message that very day! How? It was Sunday. I had no appointment. His house was always heavily guarded, and I didn't even have his phone number. God would have to do it. Knowing that, I stepped off the shore and into the water. And when I did, the waters parted. Immediately, I knew what I needed to do. I would go through a Christian friend who was well acquainted with the family. If anyone could get me in, he was the man. That day I happened to be traveling with Moses Vegh, a modern-day prophet of God, and Bill Graafsma, a pastor. We piled into my old Jeep and headed for his house. My friend listened intently while I told the story and then quickly told us what to do. Armed with his plan, we went at once to the leader's home. One door after another opened.

Soon after our arrival, we found ourselves sitting in his living room explaining the reason for our visit to his wife and father-in-law who took our message to him. While waiting for them to return, sitting on the comfortable sofas, I saw the very women I had seen in the vision walk past us and go up the stairs. You guessed it. She was also dressed in red. We hadn't arrived any too soon! God was confirming the vision. Minutes after our arrival, a large bus arrived with political supporters ready to take this prominent political leader and wife to an afternoon open-air political rally. Very quickly, without any fanfare, the man we needed to talk to entered the room. After brief introductions, his wife told him the whole story. He was visibly moved by what he heard. When she finished, he turned to me, and with the utmost seriousness, said, "Maybe I should wear a bullet-proof vest." We agreed. As he turned to go, he said, "If I get through this alive, let's have coffee." His life was spared. I have no doubt that we short-circuited one of Satan's plans so that one of God's could be carried out. All we did was get out of the boat!

You must let yourself be submerged. If you don't know how, He will help you. The Holy Spirit will gently lead you step-by-step out into the deepest part of His river where the Holy Spirit will flow around you in gentle, yet powerful movements, encouraging you to totally trust Him. You *must* trust Him. He is the Captain of your boat. He knows every twist and turn along the way.

If you let Him, He will teach you the way. Soon you will find yourself being used by Him to help others make the plunge. God's heart is always to reach others. As long as this desire moves us, we will never become a spiritual Dead

Sea. Instead, we will always be a channel of life through which God's wonderful river can flow.

Every day we need to contemplate His glory, even though when we do the feelings of joy become so intense that we actually groan, so unaccustomed are we to spiritual feelings of that degree and power. Our hearts cry out to know Him and do His will. The Lord will never ignore that cry. On the contrary, He will come leaping over mountains to reach our side at the first sound of our soul's agony. Like a compassionate physician, He will first peer inside our hearts where, if He detects sickness or hurt or pain, He will then apply His healing salve. I will always remember the evening the Lord healed my wounded soul.

It occurred during a mission's conference in Clearwater, Florida. During the service, God's Spirit was being poured out in an unusual way. As I sat totally engaged in what God's servant was saying, I broke down and began to weep. Deep inside I could sense that God was renewing my spirit, healing wounds, and carefully working into the fabric of my spirit the grace I would need to become the vessel He wanted me to become, a vessel He could use, a vessel through which He could pour out His grace to renew others. (After all, only the renewed can renew others.) I let God continue His spiritual surgery. When He was done, I felt like a new man. A deep peace had taken possession of my heart and I knew that He was in control. He simply wanted me to trust Him in all things and at all times. He wanted me to get into the water and allow the water to release my aching soul.

We must be convinced of this: He always acts in our best interests and always leads us in such a way as to take us deeper. His plan is to totally submerge us. He will do whatever it takes to lead us away from self-reliance to God-dependence. In this passage in Ezekiel, the angel led the prophet away from the shore and into the water. This is God's will for us, but we must respond in faith. Cry out to the Lord for greater faith. He is merciful and full of compassion. If it's greater faith that you want so that you will step away from the security of the shore and into the waters of trust, take heart. It's greater faith you will get.

Pinpointing your location:

Do you have enough desire to venture beyond the security of the dry river banks in order to explore the unknown plans and purposes God has for your life?

Plotting your course:

The greatest movers and shakers in the kingdom of God are people who have totally abandoned themselves to His care.

Praying in your destination:

1. _______________________________________

2. _______________________________________

3. _______________________________________

You Can't Drown in Living Water

"... so where the river flows everything will live."
(Ezekiel 47:9)

Go ahead and get in; you won't drown. You can't drown in *living* water. When it comes to talking about the Lord and His plans for us, we have to say that He never plans anything that will harm or hurt us. Yes, He allows things to happen in our lives that prune and perfect us, but not things that will cripple our spiritual lives or diminish the outpouring of blessings over our lives. Sometimes it's hard to know the difference. We need to hone our skills at discerning between difficulties that develop us and those that deter us from reaching the spiritual goals our Heavenly Father has set for us. If His road involves suffering, we can be confident it will serve a godly purpose if we view it with the proper perspective.

It is hard to watch people suffer. As a physician and pastor/missionary, I have seen much suffering. I have seen the toll that lengthy illnesses can take on a family, and I have seen the devastation left behind when natural disasters strike. Tragedy has many faces, not one of which is pleasant to look at. Tragedy respects neither age nor gender. It strikes when you least expect it and is never welcome. Its bite is always painful.

My own spirit winces at the memory of a tragic drowning that occurred during an annual church retreat in the early 90s. During these retreats several hundred people spend three days together for a time of renewal and relaxation. Swimming is always part of the event, but one particular year tragedy struck. The nine-year-old son and only child of a single mother and new believer drowned in the campground's pool. The pastor and church family were absolutely grief-stricken. The retreat was cancelled and everyone returned to the capital, mourning the loss of that poor boy.

No one could believe that it happened. The young mother, overcome with sorrow, dropped to her knees and cried when I told her that her son didn't survive. It seemed a miracle though that she did not lose heart, nor did she become bitter. She bore the pain and in time was healed. She drew near to God, and God drew near to her. She did what we all must do when tragedy strikes near us. No one believes that she should have pretended it didn't happen, because it did. Her tears were proof. The tears of her Christian brothers and sisters were proof. And proof could be found in the gaping wound her son's death left in her heart. I could not keep from crying as I looked at the expression of disbelief on her face the moment she was told the truth. Neither could I stop the lump from forming in my throat as I witnessed her courage to face tomorrow the day death tried to mock her. Today, her strength in the face of loss is a constant reminder that death is not the victor. Evil does not have the last word; God does.

Jesus said, "I have come that they may have life, and have it to the full" (John 10:10). It seems pretty clear from this that Jesus intends to bless us with everything that pertains to life and godliness. Jesus has not forgotten that we live in the real world and that we must eat to live and that from time to time we become sick. Jesus has not forgotten that. We quickly learn that He has come, not to give us a mask with which to cover our eyes in order to hide from the truth, but instead to give us a healing salve to heal our eyes from the burning and smarting sight of the truth. He has given us the Kingdom. "But seek first his kingdom and his righteousness, and all these things will be given to you as well," said Jesus (Matthew 6:33).

The way to overcome tragedy is to fully abandon ourselves to His loving care. We come to trust His person, plans, and purposes. Even when storms blow and the waves threaten to capsize our little boat, it is good to remember who the Captain is. The dear woman who lost her son may have been blindsided by the angry storm that blew her way that day, but she did not become a victim of it. Her faith and trust turned a tumultuous sea into a source of life and strength for others. Her example turned death to victory and gave hope to others who one day might have to face the same. She discovered that when you trust in the current of God's love that flows in His mighty river, you will never be overcome no matter how high the waters rise. God's plan is for you to take the plunge. No matter how deep you go, you will find yourself on top. Remember, God wants you to be a *river traveler*.

Pinpointing your location:

Are you willing to step out of your comfort zone where everything is predictable and familiar in order to step into that realm in God where new and exciting dimensions await your exploration?

Plotting your course:

When you decide not to settle for *near-life* experiences and push instead for the real thing, God will open before you the fullness of His kingdom.

Praying in your destination:

1. ____________________________

2. ____________________________

3. ____________________________

Together at Last

"As it is, there are many parts, but one body."
(1 Corinthians 12:20)

We are not alone on this journey, although that is exactly how many people feel. Loneliness kills scores of people annually. The holiday season ironically is the time of year when most suicides occur. It is a time of year when we think most about our families and when we feel most acutely their absence. Divorce takes some, illness others, and wars take countless thousands more. Millions live alone, without father, mother, brother, or sister. In fact, millions more live surrounded by people—even family—and still feel utterly alone in the universe, a lusterless piece of dust destined to wander the great expanse of space without purpose or pleasure.

That is how I felt as a young college student in the years preceding my conversion to Christ. I had a family, but I felt out of touch. I had friends, but somehow I felt we rarely connected. My heart ached with pain. Like many of my generation, I dabbled in drugs to escape a world I wished to avoid. One evening I took a tab of LSD so I could at least spend the next several hours in an imaginary world feeling good. But to my horror, what started out as an adventure quickly turned into a night of terror. Out of nowhere an inexplicable urge to kill myself came over me. If I had access to a gun, I would not be here today.

A battle for my mind and soul had begun. Like the waves of the sea, one urge after another assaulted my consciousness during the ensuing hours. In order not to lose my mind, I would have to do something quickly in order to distract myself from this raging war within my mind. So I walked the streets of the college town where I was studying, fighting these feelings with every step. Hours of struggle quickly wore me down. Then, unexpectedly, something happened that changed everything. While walking down the dark path back to my dorm, I heard a voice. It was authoritative and unmistakably clear. Its words went straight to my heart, *"Don't do it. Soon you will find what you are looking for."* With that an indescribable peace settled over me. With that the diabolical drive to take my own life was gone. With that I wanted to live! I had been given hope. What it was that I was going to find I did not know, but I knew that it would have to be a miracle.

Once back in my dorm room, I sank down in the chair at my desk and picked up the Bible that I had brought from home for the comparative religions course I was taking that semester. Opening at Genesis, I read it for the first time. I read it with an intensity and interest that surprised me. I read chapter after chapter, amazed at what I read, desperately hoping that the world actually was the way these words depicted it to be; a world in which God personally involved Himself, a world in which He cared for me; words that not only defined my problem, but offered me a cure; words that not only "sounded" real, but that also had the power to heal.

By the end of the third chapter, my mind had cleared. All the effects of the drug had disappeared and I had come to realize that God had begun the process of revealing to me what it was I had been searching for. A few weeks later, I experienced *the miracle*. I surrendered my life to Christ and discovered that I did belong, that I was not alone, that I was a person of value and had come into this world for a purpose. He would be with me at all times and for all time.

Our *spiritual aloneness* ends at the cross. Before the cross, we move through life under the illusion that we are totally alone. The fact is that even without God we are connected to others in the fabric of life, affected by others and affecting others. When Christ enters our lives, He changes everything. From the cross onward, the Body becomes our home; every member, a part of our family; every move it makes, our own; every joy, our greatest happiness; each tear, as if it dropped from our own sorrow-filled soul. Membership in His Body makes us family. Now, given the fact that we share that filial bond, it is a short step of logic to conclude the following: Our concerns ought to extend to both the youngest and the weakest members of our family. Moses' intent was to lead all of Israel, young and old, weak and strong, into the Promised Land. They paced themselves so as to make that possible. Our intent should be no less today. After all, our strength is found in unity. Wherever God's people unify, the enemy retreats in defeat. Whether we speak of remaining strong in the face of adversity or of flowing in the waters of renewal, it is, in the final analysis, a *corporate affair*. "Awaken the whole Church" is the Spirit's cry.

Jesus can also change the world in which we live. We long for a world free of the insanity that grips it. Jesus is about the business of creating those changes. He is banishing the isolationism and extreme individualism that separate believer from believer, church from church, denomination from denomination, and finally and most tragically, the believer from his Heavenly Father. God imparts to us as a consequence a sense of connectedness that makes us ever mindful of how inseparably linked we are to each other. He shows us that it is a supernatural work of the Spirit that gives us that "family consciousness" which is a prerequisite for us to experience a reuniting with the Father's love at the deepest levels of our being.

It is in this atmosphere that He successfully heals old wounds and straightens out our twisted memories. It is there that His endless love embraces us. It is there that He wraps us in His glory. It is there that we hear Him tell us, "You are My beloved child in whom I am well pleased." It is there that we lay aside our orphan's rags and pick up our royal robes.

Pinpointing your location:

Have you come to the cross? Are you willing to let the Spirit heal your old wounds so that you can reconnect with the Father's love?

Plotting your course:

It is the certain knowledge that you are accepted and loved that gives you the courage to go where you have not gone and to be what you have not been regardless of what it might cost to do so.

Praying in your destination:

1. _______________________________

2. _______________________________

3. _______________________________

Until You Are Dripping Wet!

"Let my teaching fall like rain and my words descend like dew, like showers on new grass, like abundant rain on tender plants."

(Deuteronomy 32:2)

Everyone knows something about dew. To see it you must get up very early before the heat of the day has had a chance to burn it off. Dew is more than that watery stuff that covers your lawn in the morning or covers your car windows if you forgot to put your car in the garage the night before. Dew is life. The farmer understands these things and we should, too. He knows that early morning is an excellent time to graze his herds. Cows and sheep graze on dew-laden grass because it supplies them with the moisture they need to remain well-hydrated and healthy. We are no different. Our bodies are composed mostly of water. People with an adequate intake of water have fewer wrinkles and fewer problems with their kidneys. In general, they simply feel better. So, too, our spirits need spiritual water. When it is lacking, our spirits grow weak, shrivel up, and become ill. You must graze until you are saturated with Him.

God's presence is just like the early morning dew. As the moisture glistens on each blade of grass, so God supercharges the atmosphere of those early morning encounters. The more we seek Him, the more moisture laden the spiritual atmosphere becomes. Once the saturation point is reached, the Spirit's anointing begins to fall upon us like the dew in the morning or like the rain of an afternoon shower. Living each day bathed in His presence then becomes not simply a possibility to pursue, but rather a reality to enjoy. This has been my heart's desire, to be so filled with God and so saturated with the water of His Spirit that whoever would come in contact with me would become dripping wet with His presence. Is that your desire as well?

Whether in outdoor crusades or indoor services, we witness the rain of the Spirit falling on the people. A few years ago in a small church in the Dominican countryside, we held several days of revival/renewal meetings. Each night, the church was packed. Worship flowed like a river and the people responded as a man dying of thirst would to a glass of water. Night after night, they sang and clapped and praised the Lord. It seemed they couldn't get enough. During the meetings, Nicki, a wonderful Christian brother who was part of the worship team, told us he saw a silvery, mist-like, heavenly rain falling upon my head and shoulders while I ministered the Word. I distinctly remember that I felt as if someone had opened a faucet directly over my head. The water of the Spirit gently cascaded down over my head and shoulders for the entire service. Though I didn't see it, he did. Regardless, the effects were evident as people were set free in God, some of them for the first time in their lives. The message went forth that night with unusual clarity and power.

This kind of experience can become the rule for us, rather than the exception. When we seek God, His anointing comes upon us with extraordinary power. If we were to give out day after day without replenishing ourselves spiritually, we would quickly experience a spiritual energy deficit. This spiritual brown out, if left uncorrected, would rapidly lead to a total spiritual black out. To avoid this, it is essential that we spend quality time refreshing ourselves daily in His presence. The price we pay for not doing so is too great. Let's stay dripping wet—just as Jesus did.

During His earthly walk, Jesus was no stranger to the early morning hour. Is it any wonder that He often awoke long before daybreak to seek a place of prayer? He knew it was the best time to commune with His father. Jesus understood that the pre-dawn hours were the ones most likely to be free of distractions, free of the din of hawkers selling their wares, free of the noise of donkey brays and merchants, free from the tugs of the desperate and the touch of the curious. Those moments were at a premium for Him, especially so, once His fame began to spread. The giving out and taking in is a daily deal.

We thirst daily for His tangible presence. We can just feel Him all around and inside us when we do. If you are not satisfied with a little and want a lot of God; if you want not just life but life in abundance; if you wish to experience breakthroughs rather than breakdowns in your everyday life, then try doing what Peter and Paul did: Try doing what heaven would laud and hell lament—fast while you pray. Your perception of His presence will intensify to the point it becomes unbearably painful, a heavenly pleasure too intense for those all too unaccustomed to such celestial fare, a joy too deep for those who spend too much time floating on the surface of things. Frequent exposure to these experiences is the only way to increase our capacity for more. The more frequently we expose ourselves to this, the better we are able to absorb the fullness of His life and grace. Unless you have experienced this kind of agony and found this kind of grace, you have not gone far enough in your pursuit of God.

Remember, follow Jesus. Follow His example. If He did it, you do it. Jesus put a premium on His early morning rendezvous with the Father. If He got up very early, why don't you? If that was the way Jesus kept His thoughts clear and His actions powerful, then it is worth our doing the same. If that was what it took to keep His vision and mission focused, then let's do the same. And, if that is what it took to be able to see the Father and have the Father seen in the Son, then let's not ignore the secret. We know that His power in work and word didn't just happen. It was developed through earnest, everyday, and early prayer. It's time to get dripping wet!

Pinpointing your location:

Is your desire to grow in God strong enough to motivate you to develop earnest, everyday, and early prayer?

Plotting your course:

Seek God early and the eyes of faith will be bestowed upon you. Then soak in His presence and the dew of heaven will become a rushing mighty river flowing from your innermost being.

Praying in your destination:

1. _______________________________________

2. _______________________________________

3. _______________________________________

A Mouth Full of Splinters

"Then he called the crowd to him along with his disciples and said: 'If anyone would come after me, he must deny himself and take up his cross and follow me.'"

(Mark 8:34)

A few years ago, I heard a minister address the delegates at a pastors' convention I was attending on the subject, "A mouth full of splinters." It was a moving message that stressed how much we need to flesh out the message of the cross in our daily lives. I thought to myself, "What a beautiful way to express it." The image created by the phrase, "mouth full of splinters" said it all. The man with the mouth full of splinters is the one who has done everything he could to own the meaning of the cross; he has eaten it. Sooner or later, we must all come face to face with the cross in our lives and square off with what it is that God would have us do.

Coming to terms with this is one of the keys to your personal revival. God and His will are found by people who seek Him. Like any relationship we value, and yet of inestimably more importance, our relationship with the Father is paramount. Our consciousness of His nearness and our communion with His heart are precious beyond words and must— yes, must—be actively sought, desperately desired, and carefully nurtured. In truth, we must utterly and passionately want God to be involved in every part of our lives.

As a young Christian, I was desperate to know the will of God for my life. I couldn't conceive of finishing college without knowing the answer to that question. I had a burning desire to serve Him, but how? I fasted. I prayed. I stayed up until the early morning hours praying for divine direction, for God to clear up the confusion. Had He designed me for ministry or would a doctorate in psychology be more apropos? There were more questions than answers.

In the absence of a voice from heaven I decided I would prepare for ministry. So, I promptly applied to seminary where I spent the next one-and-a-half-years of my life studying Hebrew, history, and systematic theology. Unsatisfied with my studies at that institution, I transferred to another where I finished work on a master of arts degree in theological studies. Even that did not remove the nagging sense that I was leaving something undone.

On the edge of consciousness was a faint, but persistent thought that I could not shake. It was there during college and still there during graduate school. No matter what I tried or did, that thought would not go away. Like my shadow, it stayed with me. Unlike my shadow, it persisted even at night. When I lay down to sleep, there it was, "Medical school." Was this God's will? Every time I thought of medical missions, my heart burned within. You know the feeling, that certain knowing that goes beyond words and yet is even more clearly understood. I knew beyond the shadow of a doubt that this was the road He had mapped out for me all along. I had suspected it for a long time, but had not been willing to face it. A deep sense of personal inadequacy, a souvenir I carried away from my early grade school years, prevented me from giving my all to just about everything. *Why give all when all you will do is fail?* my emotions responded. These feelings would have to be conquered. Jesus would have to mend this area of my heart if I was to succeed in this task, if I was to walk on water. If this was His will, would I be committed enough to see it through?

What did it matter that I had already spent more than six years in university and graduate school? Paul left what was behind him behind. Would I? Medical school? Why, that would require at least seven more years and I wasn't getting any younger. Each year I became more anxious to get out and get on with life, and now, more time, more studies? On the one hand, I sought *His* will. On the other, I fantasized about the easy way out; my will, not His. Quit school and do ministry. No matter how I looked at this, I knew that there was no escaping it. No amount of bargaining could make it go away. Something inside resonated at the thought. A deep-seated peace, a settled happiness came over me at the thought. Somehow I knew it would turn out all right if I could overcome the superficial feelings of retreat that clamored for my attention.

No matter that I wasn't a pre-med student in college; I would have to go back to college to get the courses I would need for medical school. Where would we go? The Lord led us to Oral Roberts University and by the fall my wife and I had moved to Tulsa. Even before I received my acceptance letter, so certain were we that I would get in that we packed up our U-Haul trailer and set course for ORU. It was a move of faith because as we got on the interstate to head south out of Chicago we didn't have ten dollars between us. God rewarded our faith because during our brief stop in Springfield, Illinois we received an unexpected gift for one thousand dollars! No one knew that we didn't have any money, but God did! Without that gift we wouldn't have been able to settle into our new life in Tulsa, let alone buy the gas to get there. The letter of acceptance arrived shortly after we did and, with letter in hand, I wasted no time in enrolling.

Those were two-and one-half of the most difficult years of my life, not so much for the academic challenges as for the emotional ones. I had arrived at burn-out. Emotionally, I had no more to give. Academically, I was at a standstill. I knew what I had to do, but couldn't bring myself to do it. As a consequence, my grades suffered and I made life for my wife, Eileen, the next closest thing to hell on earth. Then, one day, exhausted and disillusioned, I sat down on the bare floor of the living room in the tiny house we were renting in Bixby, Oklahoma, a small town on the outskirts of Tulsa, and poured out my heart to Eileen who was seated on the couch. Little did I know just how much the Lord was listening to my every word. What happened next convinced me that He is always close at hand. I turned to Eileen saying, "I would rather die on the cross than finish what I am doing." As soon as those words rolled off my lips I distinctly heard the Holy Spirit say, "Paul, this is your cross. Die on it that you might live."

With that, I died. The rebellious, complaining, uncommitted "me" died that day. In that tiny living room in Bixby, Oklahoma, a fair exchange was made; His life for mine. From that moment forward a powerful, new determination and drive possessed my soul that has kept me going every day since. Yes, I eventually did finish both pre-medical and medical school. But, it wasn't without cost and certainly not before I had learned one of the most valuable lessons one can learn in life. It's not our will, but His that counts!

That is the question you will have to answer. Are you willing to do His will regardless of what it costs you personally? Because if you aren't, you will be forever excluded from that group of people who have discovered life on the other side of death and victory on the other side of defeat. Jesus is the resurrection and the life.

Pinpointing your location:

What is your cross? Are you ready for the Holy Spirit to propel you beyond the gravitational pull of earth and into heaven's orbit?

Plotting your course:

Remember, while it is faith in the service of vision that enables us to fulfill our destiny, only those who actively and persistently pursue it will actually do it.

Praying in your destination:

1. ______________________________

2. ______________________________

3. ______________________________

The Thirst You Don't Want to Quench

"... My soul thirsts for you; My body longs for you, in a dry and weary land . . ."

(Psalms 63:1)

The soul on fire thirsts for God. Revival rekindles that fire. All of us who have received a fresh touch from the Father have found ourselves consumed with an insatiable longing for more of Him. When we attend meetings where revival fires burn, our hearts begin to ache with the longing to be filled with all His fullness. We relish the touch of His Spirit. When He blows upon the embers they become a raging and roaring fire. In such meetings, we are exposed to the passion of the Apostle Paul who expressed his desire to know Him in the power of His resurrection. Such intense passion is highly contagious and quickly infects us. Before long we take up the same cry, "Oh, Lord, we want to know You in Your fullness."

The psalmist, David, portrays our soul's pursuit of God in terms of thirsting and longing, both very extreme and powerful forces that move the soul to seek communion and fellowship with the Lord. David models a relationship with the Lord that ought to be the envy of us all. His psalms reveal a relationship of transparent intensity, intimacy, and immediacy, just as ours should.

These three qualities of spirit make it possible for the Holy Spirit to access our hearts and flow freely through us. David was in touch with how he felt and with what he believed, as we should be. When we are likewise transparent, the Holy Spirit heals us in the "inward parts," thereby releasing the River of God to flow through us with majestic power.

When the Holy Spirit accesses our hearts, amazing things happen. A few years ago my wife and I attended a series of revival meetings in St. Louis, Missouri. We spent an entire week basking in God's glory. People from all over the world came together in those meetings to seek God. This we did hour after hour without noticing the passage of time. It was as if we had been caught up in a dimension where time ceased to matter. Our hearts were filled with an overflowing sense of His nearness. The music was inspired, the preaching anointed. No one was in a hurry. We waited on God and He did not disappoint us.

One evening God's presence manifested in an extraordinary way. After we had been worshiping Him for an hour an unearthly calm settled over us. A period of silence followed. No one sang or played an instrument. Some of the musicians had fallen to the floor, overcome by the sheer weight of His presence. The people were lost in rapturous worship of Him, loving Him who sits upon the throne. Eileen and I were no exceptions. Then, as if on cue, Eileen and I opened our eyes. What we saw still stands out as if it were yesterday. Numerous tongues of fire hung in the air high above our heads, and when we looked down toward the platform of this large auditorium, we saw waves; wave after wave of white clouds of what the Bible would describe as His cloud of glory floated off the platform and flew out over all of the rows of seats. Both of us sat transfixed. It was an experience in worship we will never forget. It has forever set the bar higher.

David had his own experiences. During worship David knew that God wasn't a goal to be pursued as much as a reality to be lived deeply, intimately, and intensely in the midst of any and every circumstance. This psalm was written while hiding from his son, Absalom, who had betrayed him. David was put to the test and passed. He withstood the pain of betrayal and was permitted to see the glory of God in the sanctuary.

What can we learn? If we seek Him passionately, then, even in the desert of betrayal there will be a place in God that brings refreshing to the soul. Like David, let us press in to dwell where the glory is found!

Pinpointing your location:

Do the storms of life easily distract you from your pursuit of God? Are you committed to knowing Him regardless of what comes your way?

Plotting your course:

The deeper realms of glory are only reached by the strength of passion that is forged in the midst of the most intense personal trials. When Christ becomes your passion, even the pain of betrayal becomes a channel through which the waters of refreshing will flow.

Praying in your destination:

1. ___________________________________

2. ___________________________________

3. ___________________________________

Top Secret Clearance

"But if they had stood in my council, they would have proclaimed my words . . ."

(Jeremiah 23:22)

Far too many run to and fro, from one job to another, one spouse to another, one church project to another, and one church to another. Why? They have not heard the Word of the Lord. God's Word heard and kept in the heart gives us stability and builds our faith like nothing else can do. God's words have more power and life than we can ever imagine. The truth is that God is inviting you to enter His secret place of council.

This incredible experience is available to us when we press in to stand in the council of the Lord. It is there where we are able to hear God's words. It is the place of spiritual rest and faith. It is also the place of several other spiritual dimensions as well. The secret place is the place of prayer, power, peace, prophecy, protection, and, if that were not enough, it is also the place of perfection.

Think of Jesus. He woke up a great while before dawn to find a quiet place for prayer. There He communed with the Father, filling His own heart with the heart of the Father. His prayer-communion was so real that the disciples, after observing Him pray, were compelled to ask Him to teach them its secret. The disciples were heard to say, "Rabbi, teach us to pray." Great power flowed through Him because His *abiding* in the secret place was continuous and allowed the Spirit to flow through Him without hindrance.

This secret place of rest and faith is also the secret of the tireless energy exhibited by the Apostle Paul and of every other apostle whom God has used through the ages. Hudson Taylor told inquirers what his secret was; the exchanged life, his life for Christ's, i. e., Christ alive in him. It is in the secret place that this exchange is made. Only those who have been there can fully appreciate how awesome this spiritual dimension is.

In the mid-eighties, my family and I moved back temporarily from the Dominican Republic where we had been serving as missionaries for the previous several years. The Lord had called us state-side for a period of months to regroup and to seek God's direction for the next phase of our missionary work. During that time, God directed us to return for a season to the first church Eileen and I ever attended together in Springfield, Illinois. It was a difficult time for us, but I quickly discovered why the Lord wanted me there. He had called me to come aside for awhile as a prophetic intercessor. For the next several months I felt like Moses on the mountain top. God poured revelation and insight into my soul. In that secret place, I heard His words. He gave me songs and insights and so much more.

In the ensuing months, I saw God work supernaturally through prophetic prayer in awesome ways.

It was not uncommon for me to pray prophetically before service and then find that during the service the very prayers, word for word, were given through someone else as a prophecy. Problems and tensions dissolved before the mighty power of intercessory prayer.

It was a time of learning for me. It gave me the opportunity to experience what it was like to be privy to God's secrets. I felt trusted and privileged, humbled and blessed to have been able to dwell in the secret place for that specific period of time and for that specific ministry. I came to know what the Lord meant in Amos 3:7 "Surely the Sovereign Lord does nothing without revealing his plan to his servants *the prophets*." (emphasis added). Yet, we can all dwell there—not just for a while, but forever. Perhaps we aren't all like Moses or Daniel. Perhaps we aren't all prophets, but we are all called to hear His voice.

We are all called to that place in Him. Then, having discovered that place, we stay there long enough to soak in the imperturbable peace of heaven. Once there His still, peace-imparting voice is distinctly heard. Remember this; only those who hear His voice can speak for Him! The prophetic voice is heard clearest in the secret place.

To these individuals, it is given to "know God." Look at Psalm 46: 10.

"Be still and know that I am God.
I will be exalted among the nations;
I will be lifted up upon the earth."

Pinpointing your location:

Can God trust you with His secrets? How can you silence the voices (identify them) that compete for your attention when you are in the secret place?

Plotting your course:

Nothing will be impossible to those who abide in the secret place and nothing withheld because God will know that you died to self and have come to rest in Him.

Praying in your destination:

1. ______________________________________

2. ______________________________________

3. ______________________________________

Embrace His Acceptance

"I will no longer hide my face from them, for l will pour out my Spirit on the house of Israel . . ."

(Ezekiel 39:29)

Moses was a unique prophet who was given the distinct privilege of speaking with the Lord face to face. Such intimacy with God at this depth was not enjoyed again by another human being until the coming of the Christ, who, as the Son, knew continual and unbroken communion with the Father. It was perfectly seamless. In fact, the Son took this matter of communion a step further and made it possible for us to enjoy this same intimacy with the Father. He opened for all who would believe in Him a new and living way into fellowship with God, the Father. The clouds now no longer obscure His face. No opaque window blocks our view. The Holy Spirit carries us directly into the throne room where in transparent intimacy we come to know Him even as we are known by Him. The wind of God surrounds us and fills us. He teaches us all there is to know of Him and imparts to us a special kind of confidence; a confidence that comes from an unshakeable knowing that we are accepted by Him and welcome to approach Him at any time. Nothing, not now, not ever, surpasses the satiating sweetness of this experiential knowledge of His presence.

My wife and I moved more times than I would like to count in the first few years of marriage, but the most difficult move was the move I had to make from my head to my heart. It took me quite a while to experience at the gut level what I knew intellectually about God. Don't we hate to admit that our emotions make a tangled mess of our trust? They too often block the flow of revelation knowledge and keep us from experiencing the many spiritual realities the Lord has prepared for us. More often than not, I believed only what I could see, quantify, and measure. How I longed to be used by God to work miracles, to heal people, or do the impossible. An eternity passed before I was able to arrive at a place in God where I was able to believe and participate in the supernatural work of the Spirit, hindrance-free.

The hindrance lay in my inability to step over the sense-divide into the realm of faith-reality. After analyzing this problem, I discovered that the problem was an emotional barrier, not an intellectual one. My feelings told me that God would not back me up should I decide to step out in faith into the supernatural realm. You know the place—the place where our shadows heal the sick and our words can move any mountain.

I clearly remember the day I stepped over the divide. That day became one of those defining moments in my life and ministry. It was a day when I took the first decisive step into a new world. The occasion was the invitation to be the key-note speaker at a mission's conference in Texas. It marked the beginning of a new chapter in my ministry. As I prepared for it, I could sense that there was something else in the air. Intuitively I knew that God wanted to do something unique in my ministry at that conference. I knew what that something was; the time had come to start operating in the supernatural on a regular basis.

Two friends of mine visited me as I began to frantically prepare for the up-and-coming ministry. They could see the concern etched in my face, so they did what friends ought to do. They prayed. When they laid their hands on me they asked God to do a new work in me and through me. Apparently, God was listening. Immediately, His glory filled the room! Something literally settled down over me. It felt as if someone had wrapped me in a warm blanket. I understood what it was right away. The Lord had given me a new spiritual mantle. It enveloped me. A surge of power swept through me as if I had been plugged into a high voltage outlet. That electric charge was nothing less than an infusion or impartation of spiritual gifts and faith, the likes of which I had not encountered before. Without a doubt I had just received a prophetic mantle. God was beckoning me to step up into a new level of the calling that was upon my life. I knew that I knew that I knew that from that moment on the prophetic anointing and its accompanying revelation gifts would operate in my ministry.

None of this would have happened if I had not been delivered from the emotional barrier that limited the reach of my faith. We don't need an appointment to approach God. He wants us to talk to Him, ask Him questions, curl up in His lap, take His hand and confide in Him. We are important to Him. There is nothing He would rather do than spend time with us. His invitation is not for *a* time; it is for *all* time. The road that leads there is open and clear. The stones and boulders that once prevented us from arriving have all been removed. The boulder of our old sin nature, He crucified on the cross. The stone of weakness, He consumed with His strength through the gift of His Spirit. The roots of our rebellion, He removed with the blood of Christ. As the Apostle Paul put it, "Therefore, there is now no condemnation for those who are in Christ Jesus . . ." (Romans 8:1). His face is not hidden anymore!

All of us who have found Christ have done so precisely because He actively sought us. When we go to Him in prayer, behold, He is there; twenty-four/seven, He is there. When we extend our hands to pray for the sick, He is there. The Father delights to make Himself fully known. Once we become convinced of this, it is a short step into realms of God about which we had only dreamed before.

According to Ezekiel, the pouring out of His Spirit upon the Israelites was a sign that He had accepted them; a sign that He would no longer hide His face from them. His Spirit is evidence that we have been chosen by Him. By embracing this truth, we release the river of renewal within us.

Pinpointing your location:

Are there areas of your life that you have failed to consciously place under the blood of Christ?

Plotting your course:

Living in revival is all about living as sons and daughters under His lordship. The gift of His Spirit makes this possible.

Praying in your destination:

1. _______________________________________

2. _______________________________________

3. _______________________________________

The Promise of Perseverance

"We do not want you to become lazy, but to imitate those who through faith and patience inherit what has been promised."

(Hebrews 6:12)

The best things in life are not always the ones most quickly or most easily acquired. I most definitely prefer brewed coffee to instant, and I would rather be treated by a physician who went the extra mile during his studies and training than by the one who did his best to just get by. Yet we complain when the Lord decides we need a few more years on the backside of the desert before He releases us upon the world. We complain even though we know deep inside that the business of the Kingdom is of inestimably more importance than any other.

One of the most difficult requests that the Lord makes of us is to wait, because the modern world wants everything *now*. Two words that characterize modern culture,

69

instant and *easy*, seem to accurately describe how people want life to be served up to them. Too many unpleasant memories are associated with waiting; waiting to hear the results of the biopsy of the lump in your breast; waiting to hear if those involved in the fatal accident that occurred along the route your husband takes to work included him; waiting to hear if the children killed in the senseless shootings at the grade school were yours; waiting to hear whether you got the job you applied for; waiting for your acceptance letter to college. Sometimes the waiting simply involves waiting to grow up. The Lord's kind of waiting is not a passive waiting. The Bible-kind implies pressing ahead in faith. It means persevering under fire, maintaining hope in desperate times, and standing when others around you are falling.

I often wondered what the prophet meant when he prophesied over me these words, "You will be a medical doctor. You will be a medical doctor. You will be a medical doctor!" We had been working all day at the children's home in Holdenville, Oklahoma. It was Saturday, summer, and hot, 104 degrees in the shade. Eileen's glasses kept slipping down her nose while she washed dishes. Our dog, Muffit, spent the afternoon killing the chickens that ran wild on the property. Desperate for ministry, Eileen and I made the two hour trip from Tulsa to Holdenville every weekend so that we could be involved in doing something—anything! We offered our services to a pastor and his wife we very much respected whose ministry had touched our lives a few years before. They were the pastors of a small church in a small town that had about as many churches as people.

None of this bothered us. True enough, we were after high adventure, yet we would be willing to settle for some plain-old-down-home "getting your hands dirty" kind of work just so we could be near that precious couple. He was more prophet than pastor—a fact anyone who really knew him could tell you; a fact that might explain why a man with his obvious, exceptional giftings in the prophetic might find himself pastor of a church whose size numerically did not seem to match his stature spiritually. We only hoped that some of his grace would rub off on us. After all, we respected him and his prophetic ministry. Here was a man who had never missed it, and we had no reason to doubt that what he would speak over us that night would do anything other than come to pass. The stage was set for an unforgettable moment.

As was our custom, at least on the nights we slept at the boys' home instead of in town at Pastor Turner's house, we adjourned to the drawing room, which was, in this case, four chairs set up out on the lawn under a stellar heavens, stars shining like diamonds against a black velvet background. A breezeless evening, the sound of crickets and the smell of summer made up the decor of our sitting room. Without warning, Brother Turner, in his sixties, gray-headed and stocky, stood up, took off his glasses, squinted, and pointed in my direction. With hands uplifted, he began to prophecy, "The Lord is going to send you to a land of dark skinned peoples where you will put down your roots and call it your home and not desire to return (which might explain why at the time of this writing we are in our 24th year of ministry in the Dominican Republic and still going strong). You will minister in natural things and spiritual things, and you will be a medical doctor; you will be a medical doctor; you will be a medical doctor." I wondered why the last phrase was repeated. Was it because I was discouraged and the Lord wished to encourage me, or was there a deeper reason for it?

On the way home from Holdenville that weekend, we were in a near-fatal car accident. We survived the crash, but our car did not. Without transportation, our trips to Holdenville had to be put on hold (no pun intended). The next Sunday, we visited a church we had only heard about in East Tulsa. Overall, the service was unremarkable, except for the closing. During the ministry time following the message, while the pastor prayed with the people at the altar, an elder in the church with a respected prophetic ministry walked over to us, and from a pew's distance away, pointed his finger at me and began to prophesy. He said, "Unpack your bags and stay until you finish what God has brought you to this part of the country to do. A drive will overtake you that no man will be able to quench until you finish what God has called you to do." This man did not know that I was at the point of leaving the university, forgetting the whole idea of medical school and returning to Chicago. Eileen and I had talked that very week about packing our bags and going home. As is always the case in these prophetic encounters God was well aware of our frame of mind and He didn't want us to quit. Wow! God had my number. If twice wasn't enough, He spoke to me a third time a few weeks later through another pastor who, like the previous two, pointed his finger at me and spoke by inspiration of the Holy Spirit telling me to stay in school. I was beginning to get the message. God wanted me to *persevere*.

All of this made sense about six years later on the day the medical school I was attending was closed down. More than fours years of work in medical school, not counting the years of preparation before that, were apparently down the drain. I was attending a Christian University in the Dominican Republic under a medical missions' scholarship when this occurred. All I wanted to do was prepare for missions. It isn't that I had never been allured by the prospect of a lucrative practice in the States. I had, but put quite simply such a practice in the States was not a part of my secret orders. Leave that to somebody else. So, why did it happen?

I remember the morning it did. Somewhere in that whole mix, the Lord came to me and reminded me of what He said to Paul when he was shipwrecked on the Isle of Malta. The Lord spoke to him in the night during the storm, just prior to the ship's breaking up, and told him, ". . . Do not be afraid, Paul. You must stand trial before Caesar; and God has graciously given you the lives of all who sail with you" (Acts 27:24). You see, there are some things you just have to do. Medical school was one of those things for me! Then, when the sailors attempted to escape, Paul told them in Acts 27:31, ". . . Unless these men stay with the ship, you cannot be saved." I knew that if I would stay with this ship, the one God and I were sailing on, I would make it safely to port.

In my case, the ship was the vision, His vision, the one I had made my own. My heart's desire was to become a medical doctor and serve Christ as a missionary. Somehow, someday, I would see the fulfillment of that prophetic word. Remember, it was one of those *musts* that God ordains for our lives. More than two years later, at another institution, I received my MD degree after repeating half of my medical school studies and repeating the internship I was doing when the school closed. We celebrated. We rejoiced. We were ecstatic. This "crown," I cast it at His feet! Yes, it was somewhat anti-climactic, and, yes, we were certainly worn down, weary from the road. It had been incredibly hectic, and unbelievably stressful. Some days we had to remind ourselves to breathe. Yes, there were many days when the only thing that moved us forward toward the goal was nothing more than sheer grit. But when it was over, we thanked God for fulfilling His every word.

Why did the prophet declare three times "You will be . . . ?" Take a guess. The Lord knew that the day was coming when everything around me would be a blur and everything within me would be screaming *Quit*, and I would need to remember what the Lord had said. In spite of thousands of dollars lost, years lost, energy lost, hopes dashed, ridicule, and embarrassment, I finished the course. I stayed with the ship. So can you.

Pinpointing your location:

Are you a quitter? Are you easily discouraged?

Plotting your course:

When you take God's Word and bind it to your soul so tightly that neither fear nor discouragement can get between them, you unleash the power of perseverance.

Praying in your destination:

1. _______________________________

2. _______________________________

3. _______________________________

Cross-linked

"Now you are the body of Christ, and each one of you is
a part of it"

(1 Corinthians 12:27)

Spiritual renewal makes us conscious of the fact that our individual growth is directly linked to and dependent on the rest of the Body of Christ. There is no crossing the finish line without cross-linking with our brothers and sisters in Christ. Like it or not, we will grow most when we grow together. That is the missing link. Revival nourishes the whole Body. Mature spiritual leaders understand this and do their best to take others with them, not leave them behind.

It took several years for me to learn this lesson. We are often very self-absorbed, much more than we would like to admit, but true nevertheless. A few years ago, I became obsessed with finding out why our ministry wasn't growing more. After taking inventory, I concluded that the problem was a leadership problem which meant that I, the leader, would have to do something about it. Change was called for—change in me, my tactics, my approach to problems, and changes in the expectations I had about God. "God, stretch me!" I cried. It was time to start praying and hoping that my spirit was made out of something elastic enough to survive the stretching process, because, if it wasn't, God would be forced to take extreme measures to transform it.

As leader of our ministry team, I was to blame. Is "blame" too harsh a word? I don't think so. I would have to grow if I expected to see those around me grow, and especially so if I hoped to see the ministry do the same. This kind of insight is painful. Accepting it is more so, but then comes the healing. Accept it? The future growth of our work depended on it. I embraced it, and when I did, God instilled in me a greater love for my teammates than I had ever had before and a desire to help them grow. I wanted their share to grow, their joy to deepen, and their fruitfulness to increase. What kind of leader would I be? A so-so leader who takes the credit for himself? A good leader who is willing to share the spotlight, but is still weighed down by the burden of *I* and *mine*? Or a great leader who couldn't care less about praise for himself or whether or not they remembered his name, content to pass it all on to those he had helped along the way?

Right away, I got on the phone with people whom I knew God was using in leadership development and got their advice. They gave me books, tapes, and literature to get me started. It didn't take long. The time was right. My heart was ready. Events of previous months and years had left my spirit plowed and bare. Before long, we began to see results. As we invested in improving our leadership and ministry abilities, our ministries began to flourish. Doors opened in many communities we hadn't gotten into before. Our seminars and conferences began to impact many more leaders than before. Entirely new ministries were started. Our radio outreach also expanded in all directions. Thousands, rather than hundreds, were being touched. Why? Perhaps it had something to do with our team members who had begun to experience accelerated growth. God helped us see that the strength of a ministry is not only in the foundation, but also in the *cross-links*.

Yes, the environment around us does affect us. After all, we are seated *together* in Christ. The faith and gifts of the people whom God has placed in our lives directly affect us. Helping others develop their gifts and find and fulfill their callings ultimately helps us find our own spiritual fulfillment. Growth happens when this environment is full of affirming love, faith-filled actions, and hope-saturated conversation. If you hear nothing else, hear this: The faith of others releases faith in us while the unbelief of others hinders its release. Jesus Himself could do no mighty works in His hometown of Nazareth precisely because of their unbelief (Mark 6:5–6). If you hope to live in the fullness of the Christian life, minimize the negative and maximize the positive.

In Christ, we are traveling the same road toward the same goal. When one limps, we all limp; but, when we walk in perfect unity, the results are phenomenal! The move of God's Spirit that is sweeping across the earth today is bringing the Church into perfect unity and into the fullness of revival so that she can finish her task and hasten the Lord's return. He is coming back for a bride who has made herself ready. Let us be ready. Even so, come Lord Jesus!

Pinpointing your location:

Are you holding on to attitudes and beliefs that are harmful to the unity of Christ's Body?

Plotting your course:

If you will add to your revelation of the kingdom of God a revelation of the Body of Christ, then move forward in obedience to that vision, you will find that heaven will respond to your words and demons will flee from your presence.

Praying in your destination:

1. ____

2. ____

3. ____

When Smaller Is Better

". . . whoever wants to become great among you must be your servant."

(Matthew 20:26)

Great accomplishments do not make men great. Neither do small ones make men small. Greatness does not lie in the events themselves but, rather, in the character of the person. Greatness is a matter of *being*, not *doing*. It's all about heart and character. This explains why the Lord spends so much time doing a work in us before doing a work through us. You can't spend much time with Jesus without being confronted with His up-side-down way of looking at the world. It appears up-side-down, especially to those of us who spent their formative years being educated by the world.

Immediately after my born-again experience in 1972, I was convinced that God had plans to use me. However, a shroud of mystery still covered the *how* and *what* of those plans. My Damascus Road experience left me totally changed, intoxicated with God, and ready to begin a new life. My heart was to do something radical for Jesus, but when He began whispering in my ear to leave my country behind to serve Him in a foreign land, I was surprised by my own reluctance to respond. I was taken back by a resurgence of selfish feelings and of fear, the fear of living without and of abandoning my career. *There goes my comfortable home*, I thought. *Forget about a six figure income.* Missionary? I wasn't ready. I wanted to be a servant of Jesus, but on my terms, not His.

Slowly, over the next few years, God whittled away at my reluctance. He pruned me of selfishness, delivered me from fear, and instilled in me an insatiable drive to know Him, even if it meant giving up every vestige of every self-centered dream that I was holding on to. On Sundays we attended a large and growing church in Naperville, Illinois. On one particular Sunday in 1975, a visiting missionary preached the morning message. If I had to grade his message, I would have given him a "C minus" for delivery and a "C plus" for content. It wasn't a watershed message in the history of mission messages, but something happened to me as I listened. The Holy Spirit managed to slip behind my defenses and, in spite of myself, I found myself listening intently, silently nodding my head up and down in agreement on every point.

In spite of his plain speaking delivery—he read it in a monotone voice with the enthusiasm of an undertaker—I was beside myself with the desire to respond. When the altar call was made, I was among the first to walk forward. What I committed to was this: "If God should ask you, would you be willing to go?" It might not have been that watershed message I mentioned a moment ago, but it was a turning-point moment for me. I had just taken a huge step forward in God's plan for my life which was finally, albeit slowly, taking shape before me. With that celestial glimpse I began to look at my future with very different expectations. The things I had considered so important before, i.e., big house and income to match, began to lose their appeal—God 1, Paul 0. God was winning!

I was beginning to see that being a servant for Jesus was something exalted, not something to be despised. Jesus measured true servanthood as well as true greatness not at all by position, but, rather by posture, the posture of the heart. Many people spend their entire lives seeking to become great and never do because they have sought it in the wrong places or attempted it in the wrong ways. Many others spend their entire lives wishing to become great when they already are. They needlessly spend years in frustration because they don't recognize true greatness when it does show up.

Have you missed the mark? Did you think that greatness lay in the size of your church or salary or in the smallness of your dress size? Did you think that God had passed you by because you weren't promoted when the others were or because you missed the deadline for admission to the school of your choice through no fault of your own? Do you blame God for the illness that robbed you of your moment in the spotlight? Don't be discouraged. God does not think like the rest of us. He doesn't see the things that you and I most often do. What He does see can change our lives. He sees forgiveness where once there was sin. He sees power where once there was weakness. He sees a crown where once there were thorns. He sees greatness where once there was none. He sees Jesus where once we were and a finished work where one was only begun. Paul's words in Philippians 1:6 give us reason to hope, "being confident of this, that he who began a good work in you will carry it on to completion until the day of Christ Jesus."

He will exam our motivations and put them to the test. When He finds them amiss, He will correct them. It is not enough to do the right thing. He wants us to do the right thing for the right reasons. The Spirit of God is by His very nature the opposite of the spirit of the world. Those who walk in the Spirit can never be comfortable walking in the ways of this world's system. Different rules apply. Distinct goals are pursued. The rules of the marketplace do not apply in the kingdom of God. His kingdom defines greatness through a series of paradoxes. We save our lives by being willing to lose them (Luke 9:24). In giving, we receive (Luke 6:38). He who would be greatest must be servant of all. He who would be biggest must be smallest of all.

If you are destined to greatness, no matter what you give up, be assured that when the "kairos" moment does finally arrive, there is no force on earth that can stop you from fulfilling your destiny. As day follows night and spring follows winter, so too will greatness be played out upon the field of history once God whispers "Let it be." Smaller is better.

Pinpointing your location:

Are you holding onto self? In light of the above, could God trust you with greatness?

Plotting your course:

When you are flowing in the Spirit of renewal, you stop caring about whether you are great or not. If you will start caring for others more than for yourself, people won't have to ask if this Jesus is real; they will know that He is.

Praying in your destination:

1. _______________________________________

2. _______________________________________

3. _______________________________________

Going Beyond the Threshold

"Go through the camp and tell the people, 'Get your supplies ready. Three days from now you will cross the Jordan . . .'"

(Joshua 1:11)

L ife is full of thresholds. We are constantly crossing them and constantly moving deeper into the things of God. Some of these thresholds are especially catalytic; once crossed they seem to unleash an amazing amount of energy that translates into equally incredible transformations. It's about growth. I love to grow. There is nothing I hate worse than being stuck in the "same old, same old." Personal and ministerial advancement depends on it, although, I must admit they have not always come easily. Take, for example, our ministry's move from the large cosmopolitan city of Santo Domingo with its three million people and a sizeable cadre of expatriates. Life there was, in spite of the usual big city problems, simpler, or should I say easier. There, we always had other English-speaking foreigners to talk to and spend time with—a fact which spelled "death" to our process of cultural adaptation and acquisition of the language. During the six plus years we spent there, we advanced at best the equivalent of three years culturally. All of that changed when we received our call to the interior. The truth is, we welcomed the prospect. I was hungry for more. *We* were hungry for more. The time had come for us to cross over.

We moved to La Vega on New Year's Eve day, 1987, from a city of three million to a city of 150,000—if you counted the cows and chickens. Our first residence was the Christian campground where we lived with the director and his family who were wonderful people and easy to live with. Let me clarify; we were not working for the camp, but they had come to us while we were still living in Santo Domingo and implored us to come to La Vega, home of the camp, to begin a church. After their visit, God began to work on us, and before long we just knew that La Vega was to become our next home. After a few months as their houseguests, we needed our own space.

In due course we moved into the rat and cockroach infested "yellow house" as it was popularly known by all camp workers and visitors. The next three months were spent listening to rats scurrying back and forth in the ceiling and walls by night and sweating in the heat by day. Every day for months, there were frequent, bone-chilling downpours, leaving lakes where there had once been lawns. I at least had the reprieve of going to work each day in the small village of Los Valerio, about a 45 minute drive from the camp, where I worked as a government doctor in order to fulfill my requirements for government medical licensure. I made the 45-minute trip on the back of an overcrowded pick up, often sitting, quite happily I confess, on top of over-stuffed sacks of plantains or oranges, straddling cages of chickens and trying my best not to knock off one of the other passengers of which there could be as many as a dozen. Are you beginning to get the picture?

My wife, Eileen, who loves carpeting and air conditioning—let me not forget to mention malls and shopping—consented to all of this. She was ready for change as well. By this time, my wife had made fast friends with the camp director's wife and several Dominican ladies too. They talked and planned and plotted how things were going to go. Eileen was definitely showing signs of successful enculturation! She hadn't minded the move, didn't complain about the heat, or bat an eye at the frequent and lengthy daily power outages. In fact, she had expected worse. When the camp director described the house we would probably be living in she had pictured a very tiny, dirty, and rundown rickety old, wood-frame house she had once seen on a trip to La Vega, whose paint was nothing more than a faint memory in the minds of the older members of the community. Boy, was she relieved that we only had to live in the *rat-infested yellow house*! Now, every month or so, her friends from the Capital would call and ask, "Eileen, how are you *really* doing." They couldn't believe that she could be adjusting so well and so quickly. Frankly, it was a God-thing.

The changes He ordains often seem to work like that, even if they do come full of discomfort and pain. The very stress of living without water and lights will keep you on your knees. His grace somehow makes it all work out and all worthwhile.

Living in personal renewal builds a high degree of flexibility into our spirits. Remaining teachable is kindred to this. Staying in the flow requires it. The death bell will toll for us as soon as we think that we don't need to learn anything new. Each new adjustment allows God to possess more of us and permits Him to entrust us with new tasks that we wouldn't have been able to carry out without those adjustments. Each new task, though full of wonderful possibility and sobering responsibility, when taken advantage of, leads us to the next level of growth in Him.

Change, while feared by some, should be welcomed by us because every area of our life stands to be enhanced. God orchestrates good things for our lives when we trust Him with the process. We ought to volunteer for change rather than always waiting for change to make the first move. Change, if we let it, can be our friend.

For some, these changes are radical and life-altering, such as those faced by the Israelites who were leaving the desert behind for the Promised Land. For others, they are like the measured steps Ezekiel was invited to take in Ezekiel 47. Keep in mind that each step we take further into the river of God brings something new into our lives. We must never stay back when He invites us to make the move to the other side.

Pinpointing your location:

What changes is God asking you to make? What are the thresholds in your life that God is asking you to cross?

Plotting your course:

Be a dynamic participant in the changes around you. Don't wait to be acted upon before you act. See where God is going and be the first to get there. Your example will inspire others to do the same.

Praying in your destination:

1. _______________________________________

2. _______________________________________

3. _______________________________________

Is Your Water Fireproof?

"I baptize you with water for repentance. But after me will come one who is more powerful than I, whose sandals I am not fit to carry. He will baptize you with the Holy Spirit and with fire."

(Matthew 3:11)

When the Holy Spirit touches us, He ignites a holy fire in our hearts. It is unlike any other fire found on earth. It spreads like wildfire into every nook and cranny of the heart and is, in essence, the flame of renewal that will constantly transform us as long as we continue to welcome it.

The fire of God has many faces. One facet is that of judgment. It burns up what is not of God in order that what is of God might remain. God is a consuming fire, declares the scripture. This fire emanates from God's presence and eliminates from that presence what is impure. In fact, the day will come when all of our works will be put through this fire. According to the Apostle Paul in 1 Corinthians 3:13, every one of our impure works will be burned up, leaving unscathed only those works that were inspired by the Lord and done for His glory.

We must also understand fire as refiner's fire. Here, we get a glimpse of God as the *Great Purifier* (1 Peter 1:6–7). Exposed to the heat of the purifying fire, the impurities that diminish our faith and pollute our love, whether carnal attitudes or selfish motives, rise to the surface, where, with the help of the Holy Spirit and the Word of God, they can be skimmed off and thrown away. This aspect of the fire is always seen in revival. When revival comes, it is common to see people doubled over in spiritual agony while the fire searches their hearts. Once free, their cries of pain become cries of joy. In the atmosphere of revival, the Holy Spirit surgically releases the pent-up pressure found within the festering spiritual wounds that are found in renewal-starved souls. When it is over, the signs of the Kingdom—love, joy, and peace—radiate from the healed individual. We need to be touched by both the consuming fire and the refiner's fire.

In scripture, fire also consumes sacrifices offered to the Lord. This is the fire of consecration. The fire that fell from heaven when Elijah called on the Lord consumed the sacrifice and revealed God's pleasure in it. As we move into revival, the Lord does such a deep work in our hearts that we offer ourselves to Him unreservedly. We find ourselves wanting to give Him our all. A profound and stirring desire to know Him and to be known by Him is the fruit of revival's fire.

Once the fire of God falls upon us, we become conduits through which it spreads to others. After all, revival is not just about us, but also about others. Our journey on God's river of renewal will keep the flame burning ever more brightly. The water that flows in this river cannot put out the Spirit's fire. No one can drown in living water; neither can living water extinguish the flame of His presence.

Pinpointing your location:

Have you every allowed God to burn out of you the impurities that presently hinder His work in your life?

Plotting your course:

If you will let the Lord burn all impurities out of your life, your journey will take you into realms of God's Spirit never before visited by mortal man.

Praying in your destination:

1. _______________________________________

2. _______________________________________

3. _______________________________________

From Ordinary to Extraordinary

"But he said to me, 'My grace is sufficient for you, for my power is made perfect in weakness.' Therefore I will boast all the more gladly about my weaknesses, so that Christ's power may rest on me."

(2 Corinthians 12:9)

Day after day, we ask God to use us. Day after day, God looks for people He can use. Yet many viable candidates disqualify themselves. They talk themselves out of whatever courage they had. They become discouraged because they have believed they could never measure up, never be powerful enough, dynamic enough, or exercise big enough faith. As a matter of fact, this group of people mistakenly believes that great faith arises in the hearts of great people. This is not so. We must stop looking at ourselves and others as we were accustomed to doing before we found Christ.

Remember, God's way of reckoning things is utterly "otherworldly." What God values is radically different than what the world values. Hey, wake up! Greatness doesn't lie in the person. Greatness lies in God. Anyone who lays hold of God as Moses did or as Peter or Paul did cannot help but manifest characteristics of greatness because God always manifests Himself when we step out of the way. He cannot do otherwise. If we will get hold of Him, neither will we be able to do otherwise. We must recognize our weakness and throw ourselves upon Him. Those who have been greatly used by God know this secret. Extraordinary things are accomplished through ordinary people who trust in an extraordinary God!

The extraordinary events that surrounded Moses' life were not of his own making. God was their author. The Lord took great pains to prepare Moses. The soon-to-be deliverer first needed to be set free from himself before he would be able to do the same for others. This principle also applies to us. God did what was necessary to purge Moses of hindering attitudes and lingering character traits such as the fear of man, self-doubt, self-reliance, carnal-mindedness, and the like.

Out in the desert, away from the glories of Egyptian civilization, Moses began to see that real power lay neither in Pharaoh's court nor in the majesty of the call, but rather in dependence on God, Creator of all. Monuments and myths were now a thing of the past. Yes, with Egypt successfully removed from Moses, he was ready to deliver God's people from Egypt.

Forty years out of the loop in the desert is what it took to prepare Moses for his moment of destiny. What will it take to prepare you for yours?

Pinpointing your location:

What adjustments do you need to make in order to be totally free of Egypt's influence?

Plotting your course:

Extraordinary things are done by ordinary people when they learn to trust in the God of the impossible.

Praying in your destination:

1. _______________________________

2. _______________________________

3. _______________________________

Your Root Determines Your Fruit

"Remain in me, and I will remain in you. No branch can bear fruit by itself; it must remain in the vine. Neither can you bear fruit unless you remain in me"

(John 15:4)

The secret of being able to and being willing to do the will of God is knowing who we are in God and in knowing what we possess in Him. We are a privileged people whom God has personally and individually planted in the garden of His Love, and just as carefully and just as skillfully cultivated, so that we could become all that He had envisioned that we would become. Knowledge of this sort comes to us as we grow up into Him. That comes from abiding.

Growth doesn't just happen. It is the result of careful calculation. A balance must be achieved between all of the essential elements. Critical to our lives is the soil we are planted in because the soil holds the nutrients that we need. All things from the sun above to the soil below work together to create the atmosphere most conducive to our growth.

Many elements go into creating that environment. Each species requires a unique "mix" in order to grow. While some generalizations concerning what constitutes a healthy environment apply, certain details about each plant's nutritional needs must be attended to in order for each plant to reach its full potential. The gardener must know each of his plants to be able to create the best conditions possible. Both sun and shade are needed, but not too much of either. Nutrients such as nitrogen are essential. Water, essential to life, can kill a plant if too much is given. The same is true for just about every nutrient. Everything must be given in proper balance and in the right amounts tailored to each stage of growth in the plant's life cycle.

We are the planting of the Lord. Great care goes into our nurture. God knows the unique needs and the unique potential of each one of us. He designs the best possible growth environment for each one of us. As master dietician, He orders the food we must have in order to reach our full potential in Him. He makes sure that we receive the right amounts of daylight and darkness. While we must bask in the sunshine of His love, we must also from time to time pass through the valley of the shadow of death. If He deems it key for us to walk through arid lands, He does so to force our roots to go deeper in order to tap into those reservoirs of water found only at greater depths.

Eileen and I have moved over a dozen times during our married life. We gave the impression that we lacked direction and that we were perhaps unstable; but the truth was that we were following the cloud of His presence from one place to another. With each move, we learned a critical lesson. In one place we learned balance, in another we learned trust in the guidance of the Holy Spirit, and in still another we learned faith. Our moves were never in vain. As disrupting as some of them were, they were never without purpose. They were not destabilizing. On the contrary, they made us stronger and forced us to dig deeper, go higher, and run further than we were accustomed to or believed we could. They were good!

After all the data is in and you have analyzed from top to bottom, you can't but help conclude that it's not our geographic location that matters. It's our spiritual position that makes the difference. Where we make our abode determines the nature of our abiding. Because our abiding involves fellowship, our full potential in God will only be reached if we abide together in fellowship with other believers. Don't let that scare you. Yes, personalities differ; not every temperament is equally tolerant, it's true. Not everyone enjoys the company of others to the same degree. For some, their fellowship quota is filled very quickly. For others, there is no number too high. By nature, I can get along quite nicely with very little company. My wife, on the other hand, thrives on the presence of other people. Which is better? We must trust the Gardener and His wisdom because only He knows the distance that must exist between His plants. Only He knows what kinds of plants to keep from us and what kinds to plant near us. God orchestrates our lives accordingly. Now is the time for us to abide. The depth of our root will determine the abundance of our fruit.

Pinpointing your location:

What are you doing to create a favorable atmosphere for spiritual growth around you?

Plotting your course:

Unbroken trust in Christ is key to entering into His fullness. Only those who rest will receive His best.

Praying in your destination:

1. _______________________________________

2. _______________________________________

3. _______________________________________

The Only Way Up Is Down

". . . while every branch that does bear fruit He prunes
so that it will be even more fruitful."

(John 15:2)

It is hard to imagine that losing a ministry, co-worker, job, or friend could possibly be beneficial, but that is exactly the case on many occasions. Gardeners have better insight into these things than theologians. We are talking about the *paradox of pruning*. The theory behind pruning is simply that if you pare away the excess plant growth that robs the plant of the vital nutrients it needs to grow, the plant is then able to support the growth and produce the fruit that it should. Pruning maximizes fruitfulness, minimizes waste, and insures that the purpose for the plant will be fulfilled. It is the gardener, not the plant, who makes this call.

Our lives are like these plants. As we saw yesterday, we are the plantings of the Lord. The Lord, as owner of the field, is interested in seeing His plantings yield as much fruit as possible. To do this, the Lord comes to us with pruning sheers in hand and begins to cut away the unnecessary growth. Most of us find this very uncomfortable. When He forces us into a job change or just a change of personnel or job responsibilities, we might complain. How do you react to these words, "You're fired!," when you *just* signed for a loan on a new house? What would your response be to, "We reassigned you to Boston," when your kids *just* got adjusted to their new school? I can just imagine what your visceral reaction might be to "Are you Mr. Miller, Beth Miller's father? I think you should come down to the hospital." Your heart stops beating. Your mouth goes dry. Your legs, still strong from your football days in college, suddenly buckle under you. If you are committed to Him, then Romans 8:28 applies to you. That is easy to say, but who really wants to find out what it means in real life? Whether we like it or not, we will have to find a way to reconcile the world we find ourselves in with the world we wish we could live in. The Apostle Paul was not mistaken when he wrote, "And we know that in all things God works for the good of those who love him, who have been called according to his purpose . . ."

Let us imagine that you are an assistant pastor or an active member of your church and the pastor decides to cut your favorite program. Do you complain? Perhaps, but what do you do when the pastor assigns a person to work with you that you simply cannot stand? Behold, the pruning sheers!

We all remember growing up and what it was like to go to the dentist. Adrenaline pumped through our veins while we sat in the waiting room, hoping somehow that we wouldn't be called. The sound of the drill from the distant end of the hallway forced us to grip even tighter the arms of the chair while we waited in terrified silence. "Next," chirped the nurse. With great reluctance and near panic, we moved slowly to the cold chair and awaited the "executioner's" arrival. He poked and scraped in places he had no business going, we thought. Hard enough, we thought, to create a cavity if there wasn't one already. "Yep, there is a little one, uh huh," he said. Could he feel my heart beating in my chest? Could he see the terror on my face? I hoped not. I wanted to be brave. So it is in our adult world when we hear the "snip, snip" of the pruning shears, we react—a conditioned response if you will. Our hands fly up to defend ourselves. Our feet attempt to flee, but the grip of the Gardener makes such efforts futile. He intends to reshape our lives because He knows what is best.

My wife and I worked for over a year in Los Valerio, a small village just outside of the city of La Vega in the north-central region of the Dominican Republic. Forty-five minutes in the back of a pick-up over bumpy roads will get you there. Every morning at about seven o'clock, I left the house to do just that. By day, I worked as a village doctor; by night, we worked to plant a church. Warm smiles and affirming handshakes greeted me upon my arrival and I could count on a steaming hot cup of coffee finding its way to my desk from someone's house at about nine o'clock each morning. Nevertheless, there was a sinister side to this country-style friendliness. Behind our backs there was a concerted effort to stop our evangelistic work. I received veiled threats from time to time, and behind the warm smile and offer of a cookie was an unspoken challenge: *Things have always been this way. We like things as they are. Why do you want to change them?*

One afternoon, a kindly gentlemen who often invited me to his home and whose wife was suffering from blindness related to glaucoma, visited me in my office. Nervously shuffling his feet, obviously uncomfortable with the news he had been sent to deliver, he walked over to the side of the desk. In his typically soft voice he told me to be careful, that there were powerful people who didn't want to see me continue in my nighttime activities. What could I say? I wasn't going to be put off. God had sent us there to do a job, and we weren't going to quit. As I turned back to my duties, I was more determined than ever to not be forced out. If we were to ever leave, it surely wouldn't be because of a threat. Our opponents changed tactics once they saw our resolve. They cleverly focused their attacks on the families of our converts instead of on me.

After several months of this, we could see that we had done all that we could. We would gain a little and then lose a little bit more. So, with heavy hearts, we pulled up stakes and left town without having established a church. What would be our next move? Had we failed somehow? Were we really *called?* Have you been there? The Pruner had a plan. He was freeing us from the dead weight of a fruitless work so that we could bear fruit somewhere else. No sooner had we made the decision to pull out than God opened a door for us to establish a church in a nearby town.

Shortly after we left Los Valerio, we held a three-day outdoor evangelistic campaign in the street near our home in La Vega. The first night, no one responded. The second night, no one flinched! It was a stand-off. The third night, it looked as if it was going to be a repeat of the first two, when slowly at first, then with very quick and determined steps, a young high school-aged boy made his way to the front of the crowd to take a stand for Christ. Suddenly, with a whooshing sound, as if flood-gates had been opened, twenty-five people rushed forward to do the same. This group became the nucleus around which we built a thriving church that still stands to this day. Loss? No. Fruit? Yes.

If we will stay close to Him during these times we will grow, not a little, but much. And in time we will be able to make Him known to others in ways and at depths we were previously incapable of. It is true: loss can be gain and the way up is sometimes down! Just for the record, today there is a thriving church in that little village of Los Valerio. It takes faith. It takes trust. Sometimes, it simply takes time. When God asks you to *give it up*, He does so that you can *grow up* into Him.

Pinpointing your location:

Can you recall any painful experiences in your life that God used to ultimately deepen your spiritual life?

Plotting your course:

Dare to simplify your life. Cast off all the excess baggage. Focus on what is most important and put the rest in God's hands. Then you will begin to bring forth the abundance of fruit you were destined to produce.

Praying in your destination:

1. ____

2. ____

3. ____

The Master's Hand

"He will sit as a refiner and purifier of silver . . ."
(Malachi 3:3)

I am reminded of the words of the Apostle Paul in Galatians 4:19 (KJV), "My little children, of whom I travail in birth again until Christ be formed in you." This verse should really be juxtaposed with Malachi 3:3 because they both share this common thought; the Master will be satisfied with nothing less than creating in us the image of Christ, Christ in us the hope of glory.

The beauty of the incarnation has always enthralled me. Imagine it: God becoming man; the fullness of God in humanity; not just a distant wave, but a full embrace; Jesus, just like us, we just like Him. He was a perfect and full manifestation of God in human form, perfectly uniting divinity with humanity. Borrowing the language of the computer age, we might say that the Godhead was seamlessly integrated with our humanity in Christ. When we look at

Jesus we see God, nothing more, nothing less; not a mere reflection, but fully multi-dimensional.

The miracle of Christ's incarnation did not stop there. It continues in the heart of every born-again individual. The very nature of God is imparted to each person that receives Christ. Out goes the old, corrupt, human heart and in comes the new one created to become a type of womb for "Christ in us." Gone, the cosmic silence; present is the heavenly communication between God and Man, between God and me, and between God and you.

Your study of Malachi 3:3 will inspire you to stand still in the Master's hand until He finishes His work. Like the silversmith He is after perfection. Nothing less will do. Nothing more is needed. Modern day silversmiths are not much different than those of yesteryear. Their objectives are the same, their methods unchanged. He takes hold of the silver he wishes to purify and holds it steady in the hottest part of the flame. If you were to ask him how he knows when it is ready, he would reply, "When I see my reflection in it." So it is with the Master who has hold of us.

It is the image of Christ in us that sends shudders up and down a demon's spine, if he has one. An evangelist friend of mine related to me an experience he had that illustrates this point. Some years ago he made a trip to the Dominican town of San Juan de la Maguana. It so happened to be (and still is) a center for the occult and witchcraft. One night in his hotel room, he awoke suddenly. Sitting bolt upright in bed he saw standing before him in the darkness a man-sized figure dressed in a hooded cloak. Phil knew immediately that it was a demon. Evil emanated from this hooded figure. He felt as if a wind of evil was blowing right through him, making him feel fear and every other negative emotion imaginable. Then, the Holy Spirit spoke and told him that the demon was the spirit of Voodoo that ruled the area. Faith filled his heart. He raised his hand to forcefully rebuke the spirit. As he did, he saw within his spirit a silver object take shape, then begin to spin faster and faster while it rose up within him. When he said, "I rebuke you in the name of Jesus," the object shot out of his mouth and changed into a kind of mask which the prophet recognized as the face of Jesus. As soon as he pronounced the name of Jesus, the mask attached itself to his face. The demon, once he saw the face of Jesus, immediately disappeared. Demons can't stand to see Jesus in us!

"Christ in us" was also the secret behind the Apostle Paul's apparently inexhaustible energy and ability to ever press forward in his work. The indwelling presence of Christ was paramount for Paul, as it should be for us. Paul had a passion to see Christ completely formed within his disciples. Our passionate faith fuels the process of spiritual growth. How do we know if we are growing? We know because God can express in ever-increasing measure His life through us. We know because others can see an ever-clearer reflection of Him in us.

Within a given body of believers you will find great differences in levels of spiritual growth. Some people reflect more of Christ than others do. The more we give ourselves to Christ and cultivate His presence in our lives, the more of Him others will see in us. It is not that we continue to receive more of Christ as we grow spiritually. Rather, as we grow spiritually, more of Him is expressed through us. We receive the fullness of Christ when we convert to Him. He came to dwell in us, but not to be hidden in us. He wants the world to see Him in His children.

Striving for this is not necessary. It is something to be received. This is God's gracious gift to us: He makes His home in us. Nothing can take His place. Once we have tasted of His presence we can never be satisfied with anything less. His gifts, no matter how great, are not a replacement for His presence. Revival restores to us the desire to know Him, seek Him, and make Him known to others. Jesus prayed that wherever He was that we might also be. He loved us so much that He could not imagine anything else. I pray that we might always be possessed by an intense desire to be with Him. Personal revival causes our love for Him to grow. It is this very love operating in our lives that will insure our loyalty to Him no matter what comes our way.

Pinpointing your location:

What aspects of Christ's life are clearly and fully expressed in your life and what aspects are not?

Plotting your course:

The secret to enjoying unbroken revival is to maintain and nurture an unbroken relationship with Him. That can only come as we let Jesus be fully expressed in us.

Praying in your destination:

1. ____

2. ____

3. ____

Destined by Design

"Do not conform any longer to the pattern of this world, but be transformed by the renewing of your mind."

(Romans 12:2)

Many people have walked with a limp so long that they have come to believe that limping is normal. Their view of life has been skewed away from the truth because they have lived all their lives in the midst of a culture and circumstances that are essentially at odds with God. Such people have either not known or have forgotten that a smooth gate, an agile step, and a long stride describe a normal walk.

These same individuals often make a similar mistake regarding their spiritual lives. Having limped along spiritually for the duration of their lives, they believe that this is the way it is and the way it has to remain. This simply isn't so. Their minds have become skewed.

But, how do we un-skew our minds? How do you untwist twisted steel or reshape misshapen clay? By learning the following lesson—a lesson we must learn early in our journey. We must allow God's Spirit to fill our wings, to carry us above the particulars, and then look through the lens of His Word at the big picture. When you can't understand what God is doing in your life and find it hard to cooperate with Him, it's time to let Him take you higher. Most people only see what the prince of this world wants them to see. They miss the beauty of the plan and their part in it. It's no wonder people confuse abuse with love and vengeance with justice. You can see why some have substituted man-made pills for God-given peace. God wants you to lie down at night and sleep. He wants to help you raise your kids so that they grow up to be the best that they can be. He wants to see you happy and full of hope. His heart for you is to see you walk in His shoes, be His voice, and bear His fruit. God can do all of that and more, but you must cooperate. You must be willing to see as He sees—through His eyes, His mind, His Spirit. Abandon yourself to the current. Let God's river carry you down stream. This will require that you go against the current of the world. Stop taking directions from people who are lost. Can the blind lead the blind or will they not, as Jesus said, both fall into the ditch? Who better knows the way than the One who made the road? Who better knows the why than the One who created the world?

Truth will heal you, save you, and keep you growing. It heals your spiritual myopia, saves you from patterns of thought that hold you prisoner, and keeps you ever moving out of your circles of security and toward the ever expanding horizons of supernatural adventure and personal fulfillment. It makes straight the crooked paths of incorrect beliefs we carry about ourselves and about God. It removes the mountains of impossibilities that have prevented us from achieving all that we were meant to achieve. Truth reveals our destiny and leads to its completion. Jesus is Truth! ". . . I am the way and the truth and the life . . .," Jesus said (John 14:6).

We must constantly think on those things, meditate on them and make them a part of our being. Embrace Jesus and you will know that this is true. Love Jesus and truth will open your prison doors, set your captive heart free, and infuse new life into your spirit. Follow Jesus, and you will reach your destination.

Pinpointing your location:

In what ways would you say that you are unduly influenced by the opinions and pressures of the world?

Plotting your course:

Revival is all about being made like Him. Therefore, saturate yourself in His presence; hide His Word in your heart; give place to His Spirit in your life and soon the retooling of your life will produce the refueling you need.

Praying in your destination:

1. _______________________________________

2. _______________________________________

3. _______________________________________

Naturally Supernatural

"I tell you the truth, anyone who has faith in me will do what I have been doing. He will do even greater things than these, because I am going to the Father"

(John 14:12)

Jesus made the impossible possible for us. How many things do you think about doing every day and decide they are impossible to get done? I wonder how many times the disciples heard Jesus say "forgive" and thought somewhat despondently that it was impossible. "Increase our faith," they said. "It isn't natural," they mused. Then you hear the whisper, "Whoever said that the ways of Jesus were natural?"

While Jesus lived on earth, He did so in a body that was as human as yours and mine, with this difference: His was without sin. Human nature, yes. Sin nature, no. Jesus didn't live subject to the same nature that the rest of us inherited from our distant relative, Adam. Adam made the latter inevitable for us, while Jesus made the former a possibility for all of us. Adam made sin a chain of death for us, but Jesus made himself a chain of life for us. He performs a "genetic" miracle when we receive Him. What was natural—sin—now becomes unnatural once Jesus intervenes. The supernatural (what was natural to Jesus) becomes the new norm, the new natural for us. Did you follow that? Time to catch your breath . . . time to have your breath taken away!

When we flow in revival blessing, the works that Jesus did, we do, because He made it possible for us to cross over from the world of sense knowledge to the world of faith. Faith makes the invisible visible. Faith believes in the promises of God, and faith reveals to us that through faith we can subdue kings and kingdoms. Once born of the Spirit, we become partakers of the divine nature, and as such, we are entitled to live in harmony with God the Father in the Son through the Spirit. Though we are entitled to this, few of us do so. Yet when personal renewal knocks on the door, it's an invitation to open up and enter a new and exciting world of Spirit and Truth, a world we had only imagined before. Our faltering steps are soon transformed into a steady, forward stride.

The beauty of the Spirit-filled life opens before us and leads us into the place of victory that only those warriors known as more than conquerors occupy. It is a place of authority and power. It is a place of privilege. Now we move as easily in the realms of faith and compassion as we did before in self-centeredness, doubt, and hardness of heart.

Jesus set the tone for us. He said that He would always do what He saw the Father doing and would say what He heard the Father saying. With just a few words, He set the standard for life and ministry. Natural man without Christ could never reach it. You, left to your own devices, would never reach it. Man with Christ can reach it because he walks in God's own ability. His supernatural ability becomes our natural ability.

The Spirit-filled believer is endued with this ability. It is the Holy Spirit doing His supernatural thing, but now through us. Can you believe it? Power that works miracles through us? It is released through the Spirit's gifts and by faith. God's power can only flow in the measure that our commitment to Him allows. A deeper commitment equals a greater flow. There is no substitute for a close and intimate walk with the Lord. You need it when you're young and when you're old. You need it whether you're rich or whether you're poor. You need it whether you're a whiz at calculus or whether you can barely count your change. It's for all of us. It's time. Go ahead. Open the door.

Pinpointing your location:

Honestly evaluate your *faith-quotient*. Are you moving in the supernatural dimension of the Kingdom?

Plotting your course:

You must be convinced that He has destined you to walk in His shoes and that nothing would give Him greater pleasure than for you to be a living representation of His kingdom life.

Praying in your destination:

1. ____

2. ____

3. ____

The Power of a Consecrated Life

"I will not speak with you much longer, for the prince of this world is coming. He has no hold on me."

(John 14:30)

Total consecration is the secret that explains how Jesus was able to live in continuous victory over the enemy during His earthly life. The fire of consecration burned day and night in His heart. He embodied the very essence of Leviticus 6:13, "The fire must be kept burning on the altar continuously; it must not go out." Every time the devil tried to throw Him off course (Has he ever done that to you?), he found he could not. No matter how detailed his search, or how intense his scrutiny, he could never find a chink in Jesus' armor. No sin, no holes. Pretty simple, isn't it? Even a child can grasp it. Yet, adults often don't. Ironic, isn't it?

Unfortunately, Satan is a cynic at heart. He expects us to fail and he expected Jesus to do the same. That's what comes from walking away from the Father; you no longer hear His voice nor are you moved by His love. Cynicism is what takes hold of you when you cease to take hold of Him.

Total consecration made Jesus untouchable. Untouchables? The world is full of them; cookies in the cookie jar, your neighbor's wife, your child's trust. Jesus was untouchable in a different way. Jesus was untouched by sin, untouchable by Satan, yet made touchable for us who approach Him in faith.

Total consecration puts many things within our grasp. It gives us the ability to function at the highest levels of spiritual power and walk in His divine authority. It gives us access to all the treasures of the throne. All there is. All He is. Here's the deal, if we will close the doors of sin, then God will open the windows of heaven in our lives.

People, when they think of the word *power*, might think of money, authority over people, political office, or military might. When asked how to get it, they might well glibly rattle off some remark about "fighting to get to the top" or "Hey, I have my needs, too!" Quite frankly, the Bible answers the question differently.

Power is a necessary accompaniment of authority. In spiritual terms, it comes to those who satisfy its conditions. Such conditions are as simple as they are unlike the definitions you hear in the neighborhood market or the fast paced e-commerce lane. Simply put, spiritual authority and power are given to the person who follows God with his whole heart. It is a straightforward matter of living and loving, following, and doing what pleases the Lord. The power to do what authority allows flows naturally from our total consecration to Him. No evil can prevail against the totally consecrated life. Life emerges from death. Light conquers darkness, even the darkness of the soul. The ashes of defeat become the altar of absolute dedication.

We have seen the power of His consecrated life. Because He chose, above all things, to honor and do the will of His Father, He was given the honor and privilege of having His every word, gesture, and tear filled with God's essence. Out of the unfathomable depths of God's eternal being flowed the river of authority and power that healed the wounded heart and made the crippled whole. This power flows along paths carved out by love.

Jesus' life and person define the word *consecration* for us. He *is* consecration. Those who are in Christ enter into His consecration. Heaven will do anything for the person who chooses Christ over self, Kingdom-interests over self-interests. Supernatural favor becomes ours. Difficult things become easy. The impossible becomes possible. Such has been our experience from day one of our Christian lives.

Consecration can be increased by fasting. Fasting, as difficult as most people find it to be, is an excellent way to deepen consecration, and it brings quick results. It's a powerful weapon. A few years ago, our team began to seek God more fervently than ever before. We called on the members of our team to begin a time of fasting and prayer because we knew that fasting would be key to obtaining the breakthrough we needed.

At the beginning of the year, we proclaimed a forty-day fast for those on the team who felt led to join in it. As we neared the forty-day mark, doors for ministry began popping open all over the country. Pastors called from everywhere. Churches invited us to preach revivals. Requests to do seminars came so fast that we had trouble scheduling them all. The point is this: When we draw near to Him, He draws near to us and releases His resources on our behalf. Many doors that we would like to see open remain closed, not particularly because He is unwilling to open them, but more because we have not been willing to pay the price.

The influence that flows from a consecrated heart invisibly works behind the scenes, drawing people, persuading, convincing, and in some cases restraining them. It flows in your life as it did in His life. It flows in an extraordinariness that only He makes possible. It is that extraordinariness that makes miracles happen, wins battles, and keeps hope alive. It is time for you to discover this truth for yourself.

Pinpointing your location:

Are there areas in your life where the enemy still has a hold on you? When people look at you, do they see Jesus?

Plotting your course:

Total consecration gives us unparalleled influence over the enemy and unhindered access to the riches of Christ in glory. The world has yet to see what God can do through someone who is totally yielded to Him.

Praying in your destination:

1. _______________________________________

2. _______________________________________

3. _______________________________________

Intimately Acquainted

"Then those who feared the LORD talked with each other, and the LORD listened and heard. A scroll of remembrance was written in his presence concerning those who feared the LORD and honored his name."

(Malachi 3:16)

The pain we carry in our hearts does not need to be expressed in prayer to be heard on High. Our God is well able to see deep inside the recesses of our hearts where words have wounded us and experience has conditioned us. He knows how to reach us.

Many of us have a belief that God is very close to us. We quote scriptures that tell us that He lives inside us, but, truth is, on a subconscious level, we tell a very different story. On that level, the God we confess is a million miles away. Several years ago, during our years of ministry in La Vega, Dominican Republic, God gave me an experience that changed my perception of His nearness forever.

Because of my medical background, missionaries often came to me with their health problems. It was always a joy to help them; I considered it part of my ministry. Indeed, it was! One particular morning I received a visit from some missionary acquaintances of ours, Phil, who was an evangelist, and his wife. The evening before their visit, Eileen and I spent the last hour or so of the night talking about our ministry in La Vega and what possible future plans the Lord might have for us. It was a season of self-evaluation and introspection. We suspected God had different plans for us, but we weren't sure. We needed a strong word of confirmation before we would be willing to pull up stakes and leave the church we had started in the hands of another. We needed answers. Were we doing what we should be doing? Did God have something else for us to do?

We had felt for several months that the time was at hand for us to turn over the church we had started to another pastor and move to a new city to begin a new work. Our concerns also extended to our daughter, Katie. How would she fare in the new school we had just enrolled her in? To top it off, I was questioning the Lord about the role my training as a medical doctor would have in any future plans. After all, I felt called more to teach and preach than I did to practice medicine. I enjoyed the practice, but knew that I could never be satisfied doing only that. Before dropping off to sleep, Eileen and I talked with each other about each of these concerns in exactly that order. Without so much as a prayer, we rolled over and promptly fell asleep.

Early the following morning a missionary evangelist showed up at my door with his wife. A very worried look marked his face. His wife was ill. Her blood pressure had skyrocketed out of control and she needed help. Not wanting to waste any time, I dispensed with the usual pleasantries and simply ushered them into the clinic we had built beside our home—a clinic that served primarily the poor and needy in the community—to begin her evaluation. Once that was done, he and I felt strongly that we should pray. Both of us were well aware of the seriousness of her condition and knew that prayer might be the only thing that would save the day. We took a breath and prayed, "God, heal her. Touch her with Your healing hand," and so for the next few minutes we interceded for her healing. The room seemed to fill with a perceptible light. The sense of His presence became so real that I felt as if I could reach out and touch it. It was breathtaking! A cloud-like haze filled the exam room. The warmth of His presence surrounded us. Our hands shot up in the air as spontaneous worship flowed from our lips.

A few seconds later, the evangelist took a step backward, pointed his finger at me and began to prophecy, "Paul, the Lord wants you to know that your work in La Vega is over. He is sending you to a new place to do a new work and to do new things in you. He is going to teach you new things. And, as for your daughter, do not worry about her. She will turn out just fine and be a great help to you in the ministry. And about your being a medical doctor, the Lord says 'I have put that in your heart even as I put it in the hearts of your father and grandfather before you. I have given it to you as a door-opener.'" With that, he concluded. My heart was cut open, exposed, and healed all at the same time.

As far as I was concerned, God himself had visited me. It was a theophany of the first order. God made me feel infinitely close to Him and important to Him. He had obviously listened to every single word we had spoken that night before. It was obvious He had been present in our room. The Lord addressed each one of my concerns in the same order that I had the previous evening and had spoken them back to me in exactly the same words. He succeeded in breaking through the layers of worry and frustration that had accumulated around my heart over the past few years prior to that moment. He restored to me the sensitivity that made it possible for me to *feel* deeply and intimately His presence and to know, in the most profound way, that He, indeed, knows where I live and who I am.

This is the kind of relationship the Lord wants with each of us. He wants you to know that He is with you even unto the end of the age!

Pinpointing your location:

Do you feel that God is close to you? What would it take for you to get a *breakthrough* in your relationship with Him?

Plotting your course:

Ask God to give you a revelation of His nearness. You need to know that He is with you in order for you to trust Him with the care and direction of your life.

Praying in your destination:

1. ____

2. ____

3. ____

Anointed for a Purpose

"The Spirit of the LORD is upon me, because He has anointed me to preach good news to the poor. He has sent me to proclaim freedom for the prisoners and recovery of sight for the blind, to release the oppressed, to proclaim the year of the LORD's favor."

(Luke 4:18–19)

Everything God does, He does for a purpose. If we allow Him, He will tailor our life experiences to maximize our spiritual growth and to bring us into the most intimate fellowship possible. Not one moment need be wasted.

Even His anointing has been given for a purpose. The anointing is given for the specific purpose of demonstrating the power and glory of the Kingdom on behalf of the people for whom Christ died. In Luke 4:18–19, Jesus quoted Isaiah 61 where it is stated, "The LORD has anointed me to . . ." and spells out very clearly a five-fold purpose for anointing Jesus. In summary, God the Father anointed Him to *represent* the kingdom of God among men, which He did to a degree no one had ever done before.

Have you ever wondered why God has anointed you? It is all very well and good that Jesus was anointed for these purposes. He knew why, but it's another thing to figure out why He has anointed you. The question of "why" must be answered by each of us if we hope to deepen our own personal renewal and increase the measure of satisfaction we are enjoying in our spiritual lives.

In my case, the answer was a slow and progressive revelation, punctuated with some very dramatic divine explanation points along the way. By the spring of 1984, I had finished all the course work and clinical work required for my medical degree and was busy doing my internship. It was a requirement among Dominican medical schools that the internship be completed prior to granting a medical degree. One morning, as was my routine, I drove across the city to the orthopedics hospital where I was doing an orthopedics rotation. I was scheduled to be on duty that night, so I went to the hospital prepared to stay for the next thirty-six hours. Nothing could have prepared me for the shock I got when I arrived there. I had no sooner dressed in my scrubs when one of the hospital's residents informed me that our university, the only evangelical university in the country, and one that, incidentally, had given me a medical mission's scholarship, had been shut down. A numb, tingly feeling worked its way through my body; fear and disbelief gripped me. No! It couldn't be, or could it? There was little room left for doubt after talking to several other doctors who confirmed the story. I raced back across town to get the official word, still hoping against hope that it wasn't true. *How could it be? Would God really let this happen?* I thought. The debate warred inside of me as I drove. *Do you know what this will mean?* I said to myself. I knew I could lose all that I had worked for. I was stunned.

When I arrived at the campus, my eyes were drawn to the unmistakable sight of soldiers dressed in battle fatigues and armed to the teeth, standing guard at the main entrance to the medical school campus; a strange contrast, I thought, to the beautifully manicured lawns that stretched out behind the gates up to the administration building. I was outraged. This wasn't a country at war, let alone a war zone. It was a medical school! Didn't anyone care that I had a *call* upon my life, that this was God's business? Didn't they know that they were messing with God's sacred purposes? Apparently, I wasn't the only one upset. While I silently fumed, half-tempted to force my way into the administrative offices to talk to someone in charge, several more students gathered at the gate. The decibel level of voices rose sharply as irate students shook their fists in the air and yelled at the guards as if that would make them listen. I had to find out first-hand what had happened, and unfortunately, every inquiry I made confirmed the worst.

The school was closed and would not be reopened under any circumstances. What many of us feared might happen, did. The government pulled the charter of the university and shut down all of its schools including law and medicine. Thousands of students were affected. Childhood dreams and promising careers were among the casualties. Many lost everything; money, grades, and hope, and some even lost their families and spouses, totally disillusioned, abandoned their student husbands or wives for calmer seas.

It did not help to know that the university had been embroiled in controversy with the Dominican government, or that it was partly due to a political rivalry between the president of the university who was a past presidential candidate and the party in power. The closure of the country's only evangelical university was a terrible blow, but it was nothing compared to the personal devastation that I and others experienced. Imagine, if you will, having invested several years and thousands of dollars in a medical education that you were going to use to serve Christ as a medical missionary, only to have it taken from you at the last minute. There I was, on the street with no papers to prove what I had done, no degree in hand, no earthly promise of a way to finish, and yet I knew that God somehow would make a way. He hadn't failed me yet. *He isn't going to start now*, I mused.

God is not far away in moments like that if we will keep the channels open. The Holy Spirit spoke to me with crystal clarity one evening while I was driving around Santo Domingo during a torrential downpour. With an unearthly ability to penetrate the heart, He said, "You *will* preach My Word and you *will* be a doctor." I didn't have to see Him to know that I had just been spoken to by God Himself. The power of those words banished doubt from my heart. Hope, couched in peace, took its place.

Those life-imparting words made me understand the priority each activity was to have in my future ministry. Preaching was to be first, and then medicine. That gave me peace. It was as if God had called me all over again.

Each word He spoke pumped fresh faith into my spirit. Soon, it was flowing freely. Never again would I doubt what my calling was or if I would finish what I had begun. Would I finish medical school? Yes. Where? I did not know. But I did know that it would happen, even if I had to do it all over again.

More than two years later and after repeating half of medical school, I did finally finish. Armed with the knowledge as to *why* He had anointed me, I was ready to get to work.

Pinpointing your location:

Why has God anointed you? Are you willing to pay the price to see His purpose for your life fulfilled?

Plotting your course:

Give yourself completely to His purposes and you will fulfill your destiny. Revival breaks out and spreads because people in the Body of Christ begin to walk in the purposes of God for their lives.

Praying in your destination:

1. ____

2. ____

3. ____

His Glory Unveiled

"And they were calling to one another: 'Holy, holy, holy
is the Lord Almighty; the whole earth is full of his glory.'"
(Isaiah 6:3)

The seraphs declare, "The whole earth is full of His glory." These exalted beings live and move and have their being in the immediate presence of the Lord. We envy their unclouded vision of our Father, do we not? Their declaration seems to fly in the face of the *real world*, the one all of us live in. Yet we know that these exalted beings who live eternally in His presence cannot lie! We must take their statements as declarations of fact.

What we must come to grips with is the fact that our failure to see things as they see them is due to our failure to live in absolute intimate fellowship with the Father. As facts would have it, we must learn that the more intimate our fellowship, the more we see as we ought to see. He surgically removes the spiritual cataracts that have obscured our vision.

Every living thing reflects God's glory. Imagine, if this creation in its present state of rebellion is glorious, how much more glorious will the new creation be after the Lord purges the universe of evil and evil-doers? Can we, this side of Glory, even begin to imagine what it will be like?

One day, early in the morning, my wife was cleaning the beautiful silk flower arrangements she had placed strategically around our home. Their beauty was only matched by the bright colors and exotic flowers found in our garden. If you were to take a walk in the garden, you would see the bright sunlight reflected in the drops of dew that had collected on the petals. Beautiful reds and purples would meet your gaze while the vibrant greens talked to you, so alive were they. She paused a moment in her cleaning, just long enough to hear the Lord whisper, "Just wait until you see heaven!" Her pulse quickened. With eyes now wide open, a smile crossed her lips as she mulled over the Lord's words. *Yes,* she thought, *Just wait till I see heaven!* Truly, "No eye has seen, no ear has heard, no mind has conceived what God has prepared for us those who love him" (1 Co 2:9). Yet with the help of the Holy Spirit, we can begin to see them because it is the Holy Spirit that gives us *knowledge* of His glory.

Isaiah reports correctly the seraphs' declaration. The earth may be full of His glory, but it is not full of the *knowledge* of His glory. This is important to understand. Other prophets pick up on this. Read Hab 2:14, "For the earth will be filled with the knowledge of the glory of the LORD, as the waters cover the sea." He was speaking of a future time when the earth would be full of the *knowledge* of His glory and the nations would walk in its light.

According to Paul, the veil of unbelief that prevented the Israelites from being able to look at the glory reflected in Moses' face has been removed *in Christ* so that our eyes can look into His face. We have been glory enabled. How does this work? Through the eyes of faith the Lord accesses our "inner man" and begins the process of changing us into His image. His glory, like a master sculptor, then begins the delicate task of chipping, shaping, and paring our spirits until His likeness is revealed.

His glory both produces and is produced by personal renewal and spiritual revival. The purpose of God in both is to increase the knowledge of His glory upon the earth. Therefore, seek His glory above all things and watch while the light of His presence illuminates the road ahead.

Pinpointing your location:

Have you been *glory enabled*?

Plotting your course:

Works and words both release His glory in the universe. The works of Christ reveal His glory while the words of Christ explain it. As we step forward in faith, words and works will flow out from us to release revival upon the earth.

Praying in your destination:

1. _______________________________

2. _______________________________

3. _______________________________

First Things First

"Yet I hold this against you: You have forsaken your *first love*. Remember the height from which you have fallen!"
(Revelation 2:4–5)

The Apostle Paul had a profound revelation of God's love. He knew that the knowledge of this love is key to being filled with His fullness. Look at Ephesians 3:19, "and to know this love that surpasses knowledge—that you may be filled to the measure of all the fullness of God." We still remember how over-awed and full of Jesus' love we were when we first met Him. The experience of new birth was something more beautiful than the opening of the most delicate and beautiful flower could ever be and the fruit of it was the flooding of our souls with the nectar of God's love.

Close your eyes and remember that moment: Unearthly joy flooded your soul and coursed through your inner man like a swift flowing mountain stream. Indescribable peace floated up from deep within, soothing and steadying the new soul as it took its first few steps on the new path. How could we forget the sense of connectedness that tugged us in every direction, begging us to see, as it were, for the first time God's grand design in creation and His unmistakable signature marking everything? It was awesome! The very air seemed filled with His invisible presence; not seen, yet definitely felt, and that, with an unearthly keenness and sensitivity. Ah! His presence! The cosmos was no longer a vast empty place devoid of meaning and filled with darkness. It had become a work of art carved out of eternity by an incredibly loving God who had caringly chosen to make Himself known to us.

Yes, for me, His love was in all and through all. My heart literally vibrated with His presence. Love became not a goal to achieve or an effort to make, but the very essence of my being, the very substance of my spirit, and anchor of my soul. Love became the measure of all things and the source of the same.

While each of us is forever changed by that moment, the brightness of its glow and the warmth of its flame could wane if we were to ignore it or fail to nurture it. This happens most often when we start making small concessions to satisfy our need for control. It begins by substituting religious routine and pious sounding words for a real relationship, spirit to Spirit, with God and His powerful and living words. This transpires when we decide we have journeyed far enough and then begin looking for a place where we can settle in for the long haul. Once we start down this road, preferring the comfortable to the crucified or crowns to crosses, we are in danger of losing the fervor and purity of love's first light.

Our first love for Him is the bedrock of our Christian life. The fire of His love is the essence of personal renewal. Revival that does not restore this is not true revival. When God leads us into revival, the restoration of our first love for Him is the unmistakable sign that we are flowing in it. Once you find it, you will never want to lose it again.

Pinpointing your location:

What things, if any, have you allowed to dim the brightness of *love's first light?*

Plotting your course:

To live full-throttle in the love of God is a sure way to gain entrance into the experience of the fullness of God.

Praying in your destination:

1. ______________________________________

2. ______________________________________

3. ______________________________________

Nurture Your Gifts

"Do not neglect your gift, which was given through a prophetic message when the body of elders laid their hands on you."

(1 Timothy 4:14)

The world is full of discarded dreams and un-used gifts. Terrorism and the threat of nuclear destruction are problems of the first order of magnitude, but in truth, they pale in comparison to the problems created by our neglect of the gifts God has given to us. We should nurture each and every gift that God has imparted to us. The failure to do so deprives future generations of incalculable blessings, while doing so releases incalculable blessings upon the same.

During our years in Santo Domingo, God gave us the opportunity to work with Muslim foreign students from many countries around the world. In the early 80s, the capital was flooded with foreign medical students, hundreds of them from

Middle Eastern countries, all Muslim in orientation and culture, such as Jordan, Iran, Iraq, Lebanon, and Egypt.

We maintained an open-door policy at our apartment and often had our dining room table filled with these students. One of my wife's gifts is hospitality. She wasted no time in letting them know that they were welcome in our home. It was an exciting time. We had opportunities every day to make Christ known to them. God gave us favor with them, which made it possible to intimately share the Gospel with these individuals for whom Christ died. We well remember the day that a friend of ours, Kora, a pharmacist from Egypt, was found dead just one block from our apartment. Apparently, he was killed by his girlfriend's brothers. Once his friends discovered this, they went to work notifying their network of fellow Muslims around the island. They needed a central place to meet, to mourn, and to receive the deceased's family when they arrived. We were approached and asked if mourners could meet in our home and if some family members could sleep in our spare bedroom. We saw an opportunity there and responded in the affirmative. Soon the aroma of Middle Eastern food filled the house, which we welcomed, while we wasted no time in strategically placing Christian literature around our house; literature we hoped they would read. Amazement still fills our hearts whenever we remember those days and the unusual ways God gave us to make Christ known.

No less unusual was the invitation they extended to me to lead a memorial service at the local medical school where Kora was a student. The lecture hall filled with more than 200 Muslim students and Middle Eastern dignitaries. Before accepting their invitation, I told them that they could expect to hear about Christ during the memorial. Amazingly, this didn't bother them. So with faith in my heart I took the thirty or so minutes I had and spoke of Christ's victory over death, concluding with a few moments of silence and prayer. Perhaps only eternity will tell what the effects of that service were. Only God will be able to reveal how many were turned to Christ and away from the path of error and violence that has produced so much havoc in the world in recent times—and all because someone used the gifts God had given them.

The truth is, we must nurture the gifts we have received. If you are a believer, you are a gifted person. You are endowed with gifts and talents, some of which you were born with and others that were imparted to you by the Holy Spirit. The Apostle Paul's advice to Timothy is still good advice today: "For this reason I remind you to fan into flame the gift of God, which is in you through the laying on of my hands" (2 Timothy 1:6).

Pinpointing your location:

What are the gifts God has given to you? Are you using those gifts, and if not, why not?

Plotting your course:

Revival causes gifts to be imparted to some and fully released in others. God's desire is for us to walk in the fullness of His gifts and callings. This we can do if we will use and nurture the *charismas* He has imparted to us.

Praying in your destination:

1. _______________________________________

2. _______________________________________

3. _______________________________________

The Radical Trust Factor

". . . Then Peter got down out of the boat . . ."

(Matthew 14:29)

Trust is an indispensable ingredient when moving in the things of God because you need trust to move into spiritual dimensions that are new to you. New things are part of the deal. The stale, the frayed, and the faded are not. Renewal makes things new again. Renewal takes us from the familiar to the unfamiliar as God introduces us to the supernatural life. He invites us to a walk in the Spirit, not a walk in the park. He invites us to the Kingdom.

What is required of us? Faith? Trust? Trust is part of faith. As we respond to His words, He opens up to us the most incredible world of experiences and relationships. The unfamiliar becomes more familiar as we spend time there and grow in our firsthand knowledge of that realm. No hand-me-downs here. Nothing second hand, please. He makes us comfortable in that place. Once there, you feel as if you'd always been there. Once there, you never want to leave. His goal is to make the supernatural life in the Spirit our "natural" life and to make the unfamiliar territory of the life of faith and trust familiar.

Peter's story is really our story. At first glance Peter appears to have been a bold and self-confident man of action. Definitely a leader, he seemed to be at the forefront of everything. Peter must have shocked the other disciples the night he climbed out of the boat. Walk on water? Who would have thought? Not only had this not been done before—at least not until Christ did so—but they also must have thought it a very foolish thing for a trained, experienced fisherman like Peter to do. He would have been all too aware of the treacherous nature of the sea in the midst of a fierce squall. *What has gotten into you, Peter?* thought his friends. Amazing, isn't it, that those who are closest are often farthest away? Those who see us as we are, often fail to see us as we can be.

Herein we see the antagonistic role the *familiar* can play with faith, like one of Job's comforters who came to console, but crushed instead. Our past experience can be both enemy and friend. As friend, it teaches us. As enemy, it opposes what faith is prompting us to do. Yet Paul did it anyway. So what if it was unheard of? History books are full of the unthinkable, the unimaginable, and the unheard of. The Bible is full of miracles, the unthinkably wonderful, the unimaginably powerful, and of an unheard of broadcast across the cosmos by an angelic choir: The Red Sea, the empty tomb, a carpenter's Son as King, and a plain ol' fisherman as heaven's choice for a keynote public speaker to thousands on the day of Pentecost. Who would have thought? On dry ground? It was unheard of until . . . .

We can't allow science or history to dictate to us the limits of what is possible. Limits to knowledge are constantly changing. Although science today is impotent to grow back a lost limb or restore sight to the blind, who would dare say it wouldn't be able to do so tomorrow? If we walk by sight we are going to miss the amazingly wonderful and miraculous things God has prepared for us.

Faith allows us to see things in a different light. Faith gives us *night vision* to walk when others cannot see. Faith makes it possible to see upside-down things right-side up and the end of things before they start. Peter didn't stop to analyze the height of the waves or the direction of the wind before he stepped out of the boat. He had faith. He did the only thing his heart told him to do; he trusted Jesus. At Jesus' bidding, Peter climbed out of the boat and stepped down upon the wind-torn, wave-tossed surface of the sea. He had faith. Faith always makes things more solid than they seem to be. If we live each day with that kind of trust, there will be absolutely nothing that we can't go through and come out of victoriously.

Pinpointing your location:

Are you the kind of person who tends to judge what is possible based primarily on what you have known, or do you make room for the unimaginable when making that determination?

Plotting your course:

Radical trust is the key to unleashing the miracle power of God in your life.

Praying in your destination:

1. _______________________________________

2. _______________________________________

3. _______________________________________

From Top to Bottom

"At that moment the curtain of the temple was torn in two from top to bottom . . ."

(Matthew 27:51)

All of the religions of the world attempt to answer the question, *How can man make contact with God?* Invariably, with the exception of Christianity, each suggests that there is something that man must do. Man must try harder, live better, and pray more, or so they would have us believe. Who among us has not tried to fill our spiritual void with deeds of our own making, only to discover the futility of all man-centered efforts?

The Bible presents us with a totally different solution to man's problem. Because man is powerless to save himself (he can never be good enough or spiritual enough to earn or achieve it), God must do it for him. The tearing of the veil from top to bottom was a symbolic act that teaches us that only God through the death of Christ on the cross could remove the barrier of sin that separates us from His holy presence. The Lord Himself took the first step. He paid the full price of our redemption. He did for us what we could not ever do for ourselves.

Top to bottom—this is the way of God. He opens a new and living way into His presence and invites us to enter. Christ is both the door and the way. He who has Christ has salvation and eternal access into His presence.

From top to bottom—herein lies the secret to successfully overcoming personal weaknesses and silencing the occasional voice of doubt, loving when we feel like hating, finishing when, inside, we have already quit. We too often malign Peter for losing faith and sinking into the waters when we ought to admire him for climbing out of the boat. Though his faith did falter, it did not fail; though it faded, it did not disappear. Peter discovered that Jesus is always close at hand, close enough to hear a whisper, even when we feel like screaming. Peter discovered that deliverance from danger is a matter of *top to bottom.*

As for us, what is it that makes it possible to flow in His direction? It is a matter of top to bottom. The conviction that God has promised and therefore will deliver on that promise releases in us the faith that sees as already done what we are believing for. Whether it's overcoming depression or dissolving a tumor, we stand convinced that this is God's business. He is the specialist. The truth is I don't have to know how He does it. I do need to know that He does it. Once this is understood, ministering healing and receiving healing are all matters of *top to bottom* as we flow freely in His kingdom.

Pinpointing your location:

Are there situations you are facing in your life that you previously were unwilling to let God deal with, but would be willing to allow Him to do so now? What are they?

Plotting your course:

If we will live this day and every day with a *top to bottom* perspective, we will flow freely in the spirit of revival. Life in the middle of the river requires us to see everything in our life from *top to bottom.*

Praying in your destination:

1. _______________________________________

2. _______________________________________

3. _______________________________________

Harvest Your Future NOW

"Let us not become weary in doing good, for at the proper time we will reap a harvest if we do not give up."

(Galatians 6:9)

Everything that we sow into the kingdom of God in faith and in the proper season bears fruit at the proper time. Such seeds are never lost and in time will yield a harvest. The Lord keeps track of every faith-motivated move we make or word we speak. Real faith, i.e., faith that is born of the Spirit and nurtured by the Word, will jump start the germination process so that growth will be sure to follow. Faith opens wide the windows of heaven to allow plenty of heavenly light and water to fall on our seed thus making it possible for it to take root and produce after its kind. In time, a harvest is produced of which we will be partakers!

A few years ago during a pastors' conference, God revealed to my heart this truth. This revelation knowledge forever changed the way I was to look at the whole matter of giving and receiving in the work of God. Now, I know that I know that every time I sow a financial seed in faith and unto God, that seed will be credited to my heavenly account.

In 1975, we were living in Tulsa, Oklahoma. I was a relatively new Christian, recently married and a full-time student. Needless to say, money was in short supply. During that same period, we ran out of money in spite of the fact that both my wife and I were working. So I began to pray about our predicament. I reminded God every day of every scripture I could find promising financial blessing. I mustered up all the faith I could, but still was unsuccessful in praying in the money. God didn't even give me time to feel sorry for myself because by the time the Holy Spirit finished dealing with me, I was on my knees repenting. The Holy Spirit spoke to me while I stood by the kitchen sink in our tiny house. What He said forever changed the way I looked at this whole matter of giving. With the authority of heaven behind His words, He said, "Paul, you have been selfish because you have only been concerned about receiving and not about giving. If you will start sowing into the Kingdom then all these things will be given to you." His words cut deep into my heart; they hurt, but they also healed. In a matter of seconds, the Lord had healed me of a serious case of selfishness. It didn't take long to figure out what I needed to do. My thoughts turned to a guitar I kept in the corner. I had received it a few years before as a gift, but never really used it. "I should sow it as a seed," I concluded. That decision released something in me. Joy took the place of worry. Quickly, before I could change my mind, I gave the guitar to the brother who needed it. It was but a few days later we received a check in the mail for a thousand dollars from someone who knew nothing of our need. God used it to get us through a very hard time.

One of life's toughest trials that most of us have had to face from time to time is that of financial lack. You could be on a mountaintop, filled with joy, but let an overdraft note arrive from the bank, and you would think you had never heard of *spiritual victory*. How we handle money is one of life's great tests. Guaranteed, we will go through it on our spiritual journey into personal renewal.

It helps to remember that God's system of mathematics is quite different from our own. Heaven is forever multiplying and increasing things exponentially. Tragically, our mindset too often can only conceive of a God who knows how to add and subtract. Heaven's way of reckoning is radically different. Where else does giving (subtraction) result in receiving (multiplication)? God has sown into our lives and He *expects* a harvest from those seeds, and eventually, He expects that the one who receives seed will become a sower of seed. Undoubtedly, someone is praying that God will make you just such a person. So why wait? Do it now! Your harvest depends on it.

Pinpointing your location:

What is your seed? Can you identify the attitudes, beliefs or hang-ups that keep you from being a more generous person?

Plotting your course:

Begin to think of yourself as someone else's harvest, and remember, the return on their investment may be what God does through you.

Praying in your destination:

1. ____

2. ____

3. ____

Are You Contagious?

"Those who had been scattered preached the word wherever they went . . . When the crowds heard Philip and saw the miraculous signs he did . . ."

(Acts 8:4, 6)

Revival is contagious. You can catch it, and you can give it away. Anyone who is exposed to the atmosphere of revival will go away changed. Some will go away with the ability to "infect" others with it. To use a medical term, many of us become "carriers." Carriers carry the potential to infect others. In the verse above, we see Philip spreading the revival. He himself became infected while living in Jerusalem. An outbreak of persecution forced him to leave, but when he did, he carried and spread the very thing his persecutors wished to stop.

In today's world, the threat of bio-terrorism is real. The very thought of it sends shudders up and down our spines. Who wants to become a victim of a bio-terrorist attack? Nobody. The world wants to know how to stay well. Medical science tells us that disease carriers exhibit either no symptoms at all or a very low level of vague symptoms. These apparently healthy ones are capable of passing the illness on to others while remaining well themselves. This phenomenon helps explain why some individuals contract an illness when it would seem that they have never been personally exposed to other sick people. In matters of the Kingdom, carriers also exist; and, yes, we too want to know how to stay well spiritually. If you will permit me to speak paradoxically, we do so by being infected with the healing and saving grace of God, then infecting others. God wants us to be carriers, and He wants us to be contagious!

We see this all the time. Every time I come back from a week of revival meetings and then preach, the same manifestations of the Spirit I saw in the meetings will occur. I come back highly contagious. You feel privileged to watch the Spirit at work. There are some people who simply seem to melt under the anointing as the warmth of heaven dismantles their natural resistance. It is a decidedly physical perception. Frequently, my own body feels as if it has been immersed in a liquid spiritual fire. Is it all that strange that the same sensation be experienced by the individual being prayed for? We are, after all, conduits of grace. It is that grace that appears to do such deep works in the hearts of those who receive it. When someone breaks down into uncontrollable sobs, look for that sign that appears when heaven is at work, "Caution: Grace at work." Tears are shed, and with the tears, layers of hurt and isolation are shed. At other times, God's fire produces physical healing. Chronic pain disappears. Cataracts dissipate, and infections clear up.

In such an atmosphere people receive a deposit of grace. Like any seed, it will eventually reproduce after its kind. In other words, the carrier, in this case let us say a pastor, returns to his church after attending revival meetings and discovers much to his amazement that the same manifestations and results that occurred in those meetings now begin to occur in his church. The pastor watches while that same anointing flows in his congregation. The flow of renewal is reproduced because God has used him, a carrier, to infect others.

We need to take advantage of this powerful and profound transference of anointing when we attend meetings where true revival is flowing. We should make it a point to be open and receptive to all that He would impart to us there because the flow of His grace can then be transferred to us in kind and, of course, according to our need at the moment.

Most definitely, we should make the effort to absorb as much as possible of God whenever the opportunity arises. Our fervent, heart-felt prayer ought to be that we might become carriers of revival so that we could help others enter the flow.

Pinpointing your location:

Can you identify any barriers that keep you from being open and receptive to what God has prepared for you?

Plotting your course:

We all influence others whether we like it or not, but when revival transforms our lives, we find ourselves possessed with an uncommon desire to share with others what we have found.

Praying in your destination:

1. _______________________________________

2. _______________________________________

3. _______________________________________

Immeasurably More/ The God Factor

"Now to him who is able to do immeasurably more than all we ask or imagine, according to his power that is at work within us."

(Ephesians 3:20)

Personal renewal would be incomplete without an overhaul of our faith. Sometimes a tune-up is too little and even replacing rings and pistons won't get the job done. There are times when only a new engine will do! To receive one, you must have faith. However, much of what we call faith is little more than an *I hope so*. If you let Him, God can turn *I hope so* into solid believing.

This is an area God has worked on in my life from the start. And I, for one, am grateful. We wouldn't be where we are today if He hadn't. Every move we made took faith. In fact, every move we made took a little bit more faith than the previous one. In fact, we couldn't do any of what we do from day-to-day without faith. How do you start a church in a neighborhood full of drug addicts and prostitutes? Faith. How do you let go of your only daughter when it is time to send her to college? Faith. How do you stay on the field, persevere in your ministry, and not allow yourself to be affected by the exodus of all your missionary friends to the States and your Dominican friends to parts beyond? Faith. How do you bury a father and leave an elderly mother to obey a call from God? Faith.

Faith is something we know something about. Missionaries are not a wealthy lot, not even close. They work hard, suffer much, and do it all on less than you would ever want to work for. We learned early on that God is faithful, as He proved to be in the following story.

Our second vehicle was a six year old, short-body Toyota Land Cruiser with about a quarter of a million miles on it! But to us it was beautiful. We took it into places you wouldn't have believed it could go; through mountain streams, over mountain passes, and up mountain slopes. Perhaps the rocky slopes will one day reveal what they witnessed, faces contorted by screams, knuckles white from gripping the backs of the seats. The day finally came when our old Land Cruiser cost more to keep than it was worth. Five hundred dollars a month in repairs was more than we could afford.

For the previous three years we had been praying for a new one. We knew that God was listening, but we weren't so sure anyone else was until the annual mission's conference in Clearwater, Florida. At that conference, it seemed the time for our prayers to get answered had come. I had faith enough to raise about twelve thousand dollars in order to buy a good used vehicle. God did one better. He had faith for a brand new one that carried a sticker price of about $38,000. Pledges were taken for $15,000 during the conference. Add to that the $15,000 trade-in value of a van a medical doctor whom I had met a couple days before donated to the cause, and we were beginning to see a mini-financial miracle take place. The general sales manager of the dealership where we eventually bought the vehicle kicked in $2,000 of his own money. An office worker down the hall, not even a believer, gave $200. On top of that, the dealer dropped the price. When it was all over, I walked out of there with a beautiful, new four-wheel drive vehicle, perfect for the work we were doing in the Dominican Republic. God answers our prayers abundantly above and beyond all that we ask or imagine.

Before I left the conference to return to the Dominican Republic, I had the opportunity to thank the congregation for their generosity. As I walked onto the platform I asked the Lord why He had given me so much more than I had expected. His response was "In the same way that I have given you abundantly above and beyond all that you asked or thought in natural things, so too will I give to you in spiritual things." I knew that I had just been introduced to the God of "more than enough" and would never again look the same way at any situation of need. Whatever I ask for, I now know to expect the "immeasurably more." It's the God-factor that makes the difference. Learn to expect it. Expect to receive it!

Pinpointing your location:

Are you limiting your faith only to what you can imagine? Or are you taking into account the "more than" factor?

Plotting your course:

The greatest achievements to which God has called you can only be achieved by activating the God-factor. Your faith in the God of the "immeasurably more" will do just that.

Praying in your destination:

1. _______________________________________

2. _______________________________________

3. _______________________________________

A Purpose-fueled Fire

"There the angel of the LORD appeared to him in flames of fire from within a bush. Moses saw that though the bush was on fire it did not burn up. So Moses thought, 'I will go over and see this strange sight—why the bush does not burn up.'" (Exodus 3:2–4).

God's heroes are *fire starters* not *fire stoppers*; people who give their lives to light the fire of renewal in the hearts of people, in the midst of churches, and in parts of the world where no fire now burns. Like the burning bush of old, the fires of God today are burning brightly wherever He is loved as Lord and served as Savior. In fact, one of God's chief objectives in His dealings with us is to transform us all into burning bushes, aflame with His holiness, entirely separated unto Him, alive with His presence and flowing in His Spirit. Close your eyes. Do you see the burning bush? I do. I believe Moses did every time he closed his. I believe not a day went by that he didn't think of it, see it, feel its warmth, and hear again the Voice that called to him from its midst.

Our encounter with Christ is like that; crisp and clear, compelling, transfixing, continuous, and never tiresome. Given the Father's love for the Son, it's no wonder that He wants to see Christ in us, the fire of His Spirit warming all within its glow, constantly shedding light to those consumed by darkness. No game of peek-a-boo nor childish hide and seek, now I see Him, now I don't; instead, a visible and steady light as easily seen by day as by night. The burning of His flame deep within our hearts is an ever-present reminder of our supernatural call, a call to live a supernatural life lived out in full obedience. A supernatural God in us! An extraordinary delight!

Many of us can point to a moment in time when God appeared to us. Such an event occurred to me in 1974. The memory of it is still as fresh and vivid as if it had happened yesterday. Not time nor tears can ever make it go away. Indelible and eternal, painted upon my spirit in colors the likes of which this world has not seen, the Spirit Himself did the painting. I was in seminary, preparing for ministry. My fiancée, Eileen, was visiting that Saturday, so we decided to take a few hours out to visit one of the local art museums. We marveled at all the wonderful paintings from the different periods. Then, without warning, I had a vision. It only lasted milliseconds, but the impression it left has lasted a lifetime. The Lord Himself appeared to me in that vision. I saw Him standing in the clouds of heaven surrounded by an azure blue sky with beautiful, rolling green hills beneath. The wind caught His robes. They billowed in my direction. Jesus had His arms extended toward me. I was transfixed by what I saw. Suddenly, the Lord spoke directly to me. The communication was instantaneous. Its meaning impossible to miss. "Paul, work quickly! I'm coming soon!" the Lord said. Never before had the Lord spoken to me as clearly and as personally as He did in that moment. That was my *burning bush*. When I close my eyes, He is there. When I pray, He is there. When I think about the work, He is there. When I am tempted to quit, He is there!

The flame He ignites within us covers us as well. The cleansing righteousness of the indwelling Christ burns like a foundry's flame inside and covers us like protective armor that nothing can penetrate. It is matchless in the entire universe. It is a sign and a wonder to those who look on.

So compelling was the sight of the original burning bush that Moses just had to turn aside to get a better look. So too will others turn to look at us, to divine what could possibly account for that wondrous, transfixing radiance that emanates from within our breasts in order to see what it is that makes our faces shine like the noonday sun.

There is a longing in each of us that prompts us to do the same. We hunger and thirst for the genuine. Our hearts tell us that there is more and God Himself wants to introduce us to it. He wants us to know Him in His supernatural dimension so that not only can He have fellowship with us, but He can also do supernatural works in us and through us. No one needs to convince us that this is true because the Word declares it. The Spirit bears witness to it. We simply know it.

Once we see God perform His wonders, our curiosity is aroused. Like Moses, we move in to get a closer look. Then God speaks. Our hunger and thirst and our spiritual curiosity have carried us to a place where at last we can hear

His voice. We touch God's heart. The "alabaster box" breaks, and once broken, His Spirit begins to flow. The fullness thereof is reserved for those who refuse to settle for less. As in Moses' case, it is given to those whose hunger and thirst lead them ever onward and ever inward into the depths of the fire of His presence. Moses became an extraordinary prophet and leader of God's people. So too will all of us who likewise press into God and into the purposes He set out for us before the foundation of the world.

Pinpointing your location:

Are you merely curious about God, or are you consumed with a passion to know Him intimately?

Plotting your course:

God will do extraordinary things through ordinary people if they will only trust Him.

Praying in your destination:

1. _______________________________

2. _______________________________

3. _______________________________

Do You Need a Heart Transplant?

". . . The harvest is plentiful but the workers are few. Ask the LORD of the harvest, therefore, to send out workers into his harvest field."

(Matthew 9:37)

What do you see when you look at your world? Everyone's powers of observation are different. Some people concentrate on details, others on the broad strokes. Some are nature buffs while others are addicted to people. In a real sense, who we are determines what we see. What is inside is more important than what is outside.

I am sure that the Lord's powers of concentration were incredible. Yet and most importantly, they also went far beyond the natural, physical, emotional, and material world in which we live. Jesus saw the heart of things. He cut through the outer trappings that distract most would-be travelers to see the things that really matter. Have you noticed they are almost always spiritual concerns?

When the crowds were pressing in around Jesus (while He and His disciples made there way to a home where a young girl lay whom Jesus would raise from the dead), Jesus' attention was drawn to a poor woman who had just been healed by touching the hem of His garment. The disciples focused on the crowd while Jesus focused on the individual whose faith had just unleashed His healing power (Luke 8:45–46). Faith always gets God's attention.

What do you see when you look at your world? It will depend on what you carry around on the inside of you. Do you view every person you meet as a potential customer for your business? Do you approach each relationship with the purpose in mind of manipulating it to suit your needs? Are your friends people for whom you would lay down your life or are they people who have managed to stay in your good graces because they have not run afoul of your will and wishes?

Remember, we see what we are! What we are flows from our hearts. Sometimes we need a by-pass. At other times, only a transplant will do. Once, during a period of deep worship together with thousands of other believers, I was visited in a vision by two angels. My eyes were closed and deeply focused on loving my Lord. It was a holy moment. An unearthly silence filled the hall. The angels flew toward me carrying a golden orb. What was it? Its outer appearance did not give away its secret. That it was beautiful was beyond dispute. I was laid out on what I understood to be an operating table. The angels took up their positions, one on each side. Reaching down, they grasped the handles of two doors that opened directly into my chest. Having opening the doors, they placed the golden orb inside my chest, and then, without further adieu, flew off. Divine implant? Very possible. Divine transplant? Not out of the question.

What do you need? If our hearts are full of lust, we will more often than not interpret every relationship through a filter of *"Will this person satisfy my desires?"* If greed motivates us, then we will strive to get what we can from every person and situation. Even pastors and other people in ministry can fall into this trap. The pastor can be so consumed with worry over finances that he sees each visitor only as a potential donor while ignoring the spiritual needs the person may possess. The evangelist might become more concerned with the numbers of people who have made decisions while paying dangerously little attention to making sure that the new believers receive proper follow-up. When concern for numbers becomes greater than concern for nurture, there is a problem!

Revival takes care of all this. Revival straightens out our priorities. When we are full of God and moving in step with Him in the flow of the current of His river of love and compassion, then love will triumph. Make heaven your home and His heart your own.

Pinpointing your location:

Are you "shooting from your hip" or from your heart?

Plotting your course:

As we get into the flow of revival, the clear and pure waters of God's river will constantly cleanse our eyes and give us the vision to see into His heart. After all, revival is having His heart in ours.

Praying in your destination:

1. _______________________________________

2. _______________________________________

3. _______________________________________

Escaping Earth's Orbit

"From the days of John the Baptist until now, the kingdom of heaven has been forcefully advancing, and forceful men lay hold of it."

(Matthew 11:12)

The deeper I go in the river of revival and the higher I climb in the tower of faith, the more I grasp that there is absolutely no room for passive believing. It you wish to escape earth's orbit you must achieve escape velocity. That requires the exercise of aggressive faith, faith that is active and tenacious. Faith lays hold of its object and does not let go. The deeper realms in God are reserved for those who are willing to press in for them. The high places in God are where you will find that flow of the Spirit which produces the miraculous in our lives. To get there, you must be violent in your faith.

The Lord refuses to cast pearls before swine, and He most certainly won't entrust the fullness of the "powers of the age to come" into the hands of people who treat them with indifference. He is calling us to climb the tree as Zacchaeus did in order to get a glimpse of Jesus. The best glimpses of Jesus are always reserved for those who will not to be limited by the vision of others. The Holy Spirit inside us tells us to make the climb and that it will be worth it. Indeed, it always is. One glimpse of Jesus removes the effects of stress. The pain of the climb gives way to the pleasure of His presence.

The women with the issue of blood laid hold of the powers of the age to come. One thing becomes abundantly clear when we read through scripture, faith commands God's attention. It draws out God's power like a magnet attracts iron. Consider the woman with the issue of blood; her case is a perfect example. In Mark 5:28–34, the woman, moved by faith, touched the hem of His garment. Immediately, His power flowed into her and healed her, as it is recorded in verse 30, "At once Jesus realized that power had gone out from him." Why did it flow? She had faith! Verse 34 declares, "Daughter, your faith has healed you." When He detects faith, He will move mountains to answer it.

This woman did not let religious convention stop her. The requirements of the Law forbade her from mixing in human company because of the nature of her problem. Jesus made compassionate healing a higher priority than legalistic obedience to the letter of the Law. Her quest for deliverance came to an end in Jesus. Jesus is always the end of suffering for those who lay hold of Him in faith. Jesus is often very close to us, as He was in the case of this persistent woman. Unlike her, we fail to lay hold of Him. She determined to flaunt tradition, risk exile, and ignore the press of people all around Jesus in order to enter into His presence.

As in her day, so, too, today, there are many *religious people* surrounding Jesus who make it doubly difficult to get to Him. These religious types want to lay out a list of requirements for us to meet in order to "qualify" to meet Him. Such individuals stifle the flow of revival and make it nearly impossible for those who want to get into God's river to do so. They always want to do things the same way. Order becomes their god. The very order they preserve prevents people from getting into the presence of God. They never would have allowed the man to be let down through the roof in order to get to Jesus, nor would they have allowed Jesus to have spoken with the woman at the well. After all, it wouldn't have been proper. Jesus always puts people ahead of what is proper.

Pinpointing your location:

Are you willing to break with tradition in order to get your breakthrough? Are you ready to escape the pull of earthly ways in order to obtain Kingdom blessings?

Plotting your course:

The deeper realms in God are there to be discovered by all His children. You must fervently seek them. He will not deny you. We must press in to where He is and refuse to be pushed back out.

Praying in your destination:

1. _______________________________________

2. _______________________________________

3. _______________________________________

Eternal Combustion

". . . Though outwardly we are wasting away, yet inwardly we are being renewed day by day."

(2 Corinthians 4:16–18)

Science has always had its Holy Grails; the perpetual motion machine, time travel, an inexhaustible source of energy—just to mention a few surely the stuff of science fiction. Every day the limits of our imagination are pushed even further. Science is on the verge of discoveries that could (if correctly applied) literally transform our world for the better if it weren't for morally crippled modern man.

The Apostle Paul spoke of a very different kind of energy and a very different kind of transformation. Look at his words in 2 Corinthians 4:16–18. Meditate on them. Muse over them. Make them a part of the warp and woof of your spirit-man. Take this awesome declaration in 2 Corinthians 3:18 to heart, "And we, who with unveiled faces all reflect the Lord's glory, are being transformed into his likeness with ever-increasing glory, which comes from the Lord, who is the Spirit." Revival stirs us to the core and creates in us an indescribably intense desire for the Holy Spirit to work in us. Each day we go deeper. His work in us grows in its scope. Our daily renewal means that each day we are changed just a little bit more into His likeness.

The old adage, "You never step into the same river twice," is true. The constant flow of water in the river of God insures that there will be constant new-ness. Each day brings with it something fresh in the Lord. The bottom line is this: If you want personal renewal, you must constantly move forward in the things of God. Never be satisfied with the progress made to date. Say no to the temptation to stay the Potter's hand. Ignore the tempter's tease to turn aside for awhile. We instinctively know that remaining where we are will lead to spiritual stagnation and death.

The flow of fresh water introduces into our lives fresh revelation. Insight from above gives us light here below. A revealed word imbues us with an indomitable hope about the future because we know that if God is still speaking to us He has plans to keep walking with us into the great possibilities held in reserve for those of us who dare to move forward into God's tomorrow.

Fresh water keeps us filled with compassion. It prevents us from falling victim to what I call the "compassion crash." Caring turns to crushing and then to crashing when we try to live life His way without His renewing presence constantly regenerating the love from above. The love for souls is continually generated. God sends a constant stream of people into our lives whom He would use to speak to us and to whom He would have us speak. He orders our steps in such a way as to lead us through experiences designed to mark us for Him and His kingdom.

Because of constant renewal, we are able to see deeper into His Word. The murkiness of the mirror is diminished bit by bit, allowing us to see His face with fewer distortions. Freed from deceptions, we find ourselves in possession of the courage necessary to look (without turning away) into His face, meet His gaze and hold it, and feel His love and give it.

We find new strength when we are weak, avoiding the spiritual fatigue that often ensnares those who travel on this road. Having begun in the Spirit, we want to do whatever it takes to avoid ending up in the flesh.

The wise traveler learns to do this. He uses the force of the current to propel him forward in God. He stays the course in unbroken communion with the Lord because he always moves with Him. The traveler merges with the flow. The believer, because he is one with the Lord, discovers that his deepest desire is to move only when He moves, speak only when He speaks, and do only what he sees God doing.

Pinpointing your location:

Where is your focus? Do you focus more on the outer man that is wasting away than on the inner man that is in a process of constant renewal?

Plotting your course:

You cannot begin to live for God until you begin to live in God. The secret for constant renewal is the resurrection life.

Praying in your destination:

1. _______________________________________

2. _______________________________________

3. _______________________________________

Stay Connected

"I am the vine; you are the branches. If a man remains in me and I in him, he will bear much fruit; apart from me you can do nothing."

(John 15:5)

Staying connected is the way to insure that we will stay in the flow—in other words, to abide in Him. Abiding requires trust. Faith is trust in action. Trust leads to rest, and rest causes us to remain in His presence. Think about what Jesus said in John 15:5, "I am the vine; you are the branches. If a man remains in me and I in him, he will bear much fruit; apart from me you can do nothing." It's self-explanatory and very simple; follow Him every day and your branches will always be full of fruit regardless of the weather. Frost will not come near you; neither will the pestilence. When others are withering, you will flourish. When others are fainting beneath a brutal sun, you will stand strong enjoying a cool breeze and welcome shade.

"Abiding in Him" means to remain connected to Him. Through faith in Christ we become one with Him. Abiding should not be confused with passivity, because faith is active. It presupposes that we will chase Him as the hound chases the hare. There is no room for laziness in our spiritual walk. Herein lays a paradox; while this relationship of abiding is something you must work at (nurture if you will), it is also something you can only receive as a gift. While you must reach for it (as you reach for anything you truly want), it is God who puts it within your grasp. Finally, while you must desire it (desire is key), in the end it is He who is at work in you both to do and to will.

Elisha knew how to stay connected. His case is such a perfect illustration of this principle (2 Kings 2). Just observe him. He refused to leave Elijah's side, not even for a moment. Instinctively, his spiritual senses alerted him. Clearly, he knew that staying connected to Elijah was the only way he would ever come into the greater realm of anointing and ministry he so desired. Elisha saw that he would have to resist any effort anyone, even Elijah, would make to stop him.

Often, well meaning people are unwittingly used by the enemy of our destiny to discourage us. They say things like "It's unnatural to pray so much," or "You don't have to go to so many meetings; God understands." Pious platitudes. Venomous verbiage. Shiny, but sharp. Daring, but deadly. The truth is, once your heart has been set ablaze, you can't be stopped. Nothing in this world can force you to disconnect. If you have been revived, rescued from your spiritual dryness, you will understand exactly what I mean. When we left the calm shores of predictability and set sail for the uncommon, the unknown, few who stood by us understood.

Behind their smiles were questioning eyes. The volume of their unspoken doubts drowned out the din of their forced and somewhat feigned farewells. Some knew. They understood. We couldn't stay. Our connectedness depended on it. The future of our happiness lay in His design. It didn't matter that we had never foreseen the outcome. Never in my wildest dreams had I imagined a life carved out by grace in a faraway place. Not once did I predict that the land Columbus discovered would be the land where I discovered God's new world for me; that the land of my death (in Him) would be the land of my daughter's birth.

Being connected is a relationship that grows as we grow in His Word and our obedience to Him. We must nurture it from the cradle to the cross. We must do so by standing with the King. He becomes our top priority, to make Him known our chief ambition. Bear much fruit? In Him, anything is possible.

Pinpointing your location:

Have you cut the ties that prevent you from connecting to your destiny?

Plotting your course:

It is all about knowing and loving Jesus on a consistent basis. Love is in it for the long haul. This is the essence of revival and the source of true strength.

Praying in your destination:

1. _______________________________

2. _______________________________

3. _______________________________

Flow in the Favor of God

". . . On him God the Father has placed his seal of approval."

(John 6:27)

Jesus spoke these words about Himself. He knew His position before the Father and was confident in it. Had he not been confident in it, He would not have been able to do what He did. Confidence in our relationship with the Lord makes it possible for us to totally open ourselves to Him. Such complete openness must exist for there to be a full surrender and a full manifestation of God's person here on earth through us.

Jesus, at the deepest level of His being, understood where He had come from and where He was going. Identity crises were foreign to Him. As He grew in knowledge of himself and of the Father, He embraced it because He could not stop being what He was: He was the truth. He and the truth were one. It was His purpose to do the Father's will since it was also His own.

There was never a moment when He did otherwise; He knew no sin. The perfect union He enjoyed with Him was reflected in everything He said and did. That the Father was pleased with the Son was evident from the beginning. When Jesus was baptized at the Jordan River, as He came up out of the water, the Father's voice was heard to say "This is my Son whom I love; with him I am well pleased (Matthew 3:17)." The Son did not have to struggle with feelings of condemnation or spiritual unworthiness. He was free from sin and free from sin-consciousness.

When the memory of sins from the past (distant or recent) intrudes into our consciousness, the sense of spiritual security that we enjoyed in our relationship with the Father begins to ebb. Our confidence is weakened. Our faith falters because this "unwelcome visitor" undermines the foundation of our feelings of being loved and welcomed by the Father. The emotional turmoil that follows rocks our trust in Christ's finished work on the cross. In spite of the fact that our salvation is based on faith and grace, when the winds of a fierce emotional storm begin to blow, it would be rare that even the strongest among us would not find their trust strained under that stress. Our memory of things we have done wrong in the past, unless we put them under the blood of Christ, have the potential of making us feel like second-class citizens of heaven, unworthy sons and unworthy opponents of the enemy of our souls who ever seeks to gain advantage over us. We must have an unshakeable belief that the Father genuinely accepts us as His legitimate sons and daughters in order for us to be able to act with the boldness that overcoming evil and representing His eternal kingdom requires.

We must come to that place of unshakeable confidence in which we know that the Father has also placed His seal of approval upon us who have come to trust in Christ. Flowing in God's favor gives us rest from our own labor.

Pinpointing your location:

Are you desperate for approval or confident in it?

Plotting your course:

The person who possesses this cannot be deterred from his course. Revival restores to us this belief and sees to it that it becomes a part of the very fabric of our being.

Praying in your destination:

1. ____

2. ____

3. ____

Supercharge Your World

"He could not do any miracles there, except lay his hands on a few sick people and heal them. And he was amazed at their lack of faith."

(Mark 6:5–6)

Have you ever considered just how great an impact the quality of the atmosphere and environment has on our overall state of health? When pollutants occupy the space that our clean air should, our bodies are affected. Cancers, tumors, and a myriad of other medical conditions can be caused by pollutants in our environment. Just the other day, I heard of a young mother who was diagnosed with a chronic lung condition resulting from her constant exposure to the pollutants in the air that blew into her home from a car body paint shop next door. She was told that if the shop didn't close she would have to move. Good atmosphere involves much more than the absence of harmful physical elements and the presence of good ones like oxygen, carbon dioxide, and nitrogen. It also has to do with emotions, words, and the realm of faith. When people speak words of encouragement, we feel encouraged. When we see a smile, we are made happier! It works that way. However, when others begin spewing out hate-filled and belittling words, our buoyant spirit starts to sink while our confident attitude takes a "turn south." Our ability to rise above these assaults depends on our own inner resources of faith.

Atmosphere couldn't be any more important than it is for the release of our own faith like that "electric" something you feel when you are with many other faith-filled believers. It's explosive. Instead of small steps forward, our faith makes quantum leaps. It grows stronger and moves to take on bigger challenges. Prayers for healing are answered with ease because faith begets more faith, while doubt begets doubt. Why do so many fail to receive what they ask for from God? Because they have systematically sabotaged what faith they had by listening to tales of disgruntled travelers who have lost both their will and their way. God does not reward doubt, but faith.

It's impossible to fill your mind with a steady diet of cynicism and sarcasm and expect your spiritual life to flourish. To keep the constant company of people who speak of doubt as if it were a virtue and whose idea of a promise kept is a promise broken will rob us of our spiritual preparedness. Should we then be surprised if our faith should fail to rally when we need it most?

God offers us help, but will not force us to take it. We must meet the conditions. His Word couldn't be clearer that He heals the sick, but will He make you accept it? No. Nothing would delight the Lord more than to perform His miracles on your behalf, but you must believe. Belief is something you must nurture in yourself and in those around you because the display of God's power and glory often depends directly on the collective faith of those in whose midst the healings or miracles are to take place.

A perfect illustration of this is found in the situation Jesus faced in Nazareth. Look at the record in Mark 6:5, "He could not do any miracles there, except lay his hands on a few sick people and heal them." There the people that knew Him longest knew Him least! Perhaps countless millions sit in absolute complacency, convinced they know all there is to know about this Jesus, when in truth they don't know Him at all. They failed to see His royal heart beating beneath a commoner's robe. They failed to hear a King's voice through His Galilean accent. They failed to identify the marks of a conqueror gilded in crimson hidden beneath His tattered shroud and under the hammer's blow. Jesus knew the score. He knew them. He knows us. As it was in Mark 6:6 so is it today, too often true, "And he was amazed at their lack of faith . . ."

An atmosphere of faith will cause revival to flow. We have seen this to be true countless times. Because this principle is a spiritual reality that must be reckoned with (and ignored at our own peril), whenever we find weak faith we strengthen it. Such is our approach when we go into a church for several days of meetings. We frequently find the churches we visit in dire straights spiritually and very much in need of revival. The people are as cold as ice and just as unresponsive; Pentecostal on paper, but not in power. When I preach the first evening, I apply the fire of the Holy Spirit and start the thawing process. By the second night, signs of life peep through, smiles appear, and people start singing. A head nods in friendly greeting while another bows in fervent and honest prayer. Then there are the warm handshakes and heartfelt hugs that were conspicuously absent before. When the altar call is given, the seats empty out as the people come forward for simply more. The third evening customarily is a glorious time of celebration and anointed ministry. Even before the service starts, people are visibly hungry for more of God. They smile and hug and praise the Lord. Like little fledglings waiting for the mother bird to return, they sit with upturned heads and open mouths, eager to receive. Faith has been released. The lost come to Christ and the sick are healed.

Revival and faith flow once we create an atmosphere conducive to them. You must work at creating this kind of atmosphere in your life if you hope to live each day to the fullest. Supercharge your world with the God-kind of faith and see what God-sized miracles take place.

Pinpointing your location:

Are you willing to risk looking ridiculous if that is what it takes for you to act in faith?

Plotting your course:

Faith is that force in the universe that can actually make demands on the power of God. Revival will unleash the flow of God's power because revival releases faith.

Praying in your destination:

1. ___________________________________

2. ___________________________________

3. ___________________________________

Fight for Your Destiny: God Does

"Though I walk in the midst of trouble, you preserve my life; you stretch out your hand against the anger of my foes, with your right hand you save me. The LORD will fulfill his purpose for me."

(Psalms 138:7–8)

Life would never seem purposeless again, I thought to myself, as I left the hospital. How could I have been so careless? It is surprising how much can happen in twenty-four hours: Fortunes can be won and lost, wars started and ended, or, as in my case, a foolish mind turned into a less foolish one.

My brush with death was so close that I could feel its clammy touch on my arm and its cold breath on my neck. How little did I see then just how I would have lost had I died that night. My survival was a victory, although it hardly felt like one. The shout of victory rang hollow like an echo deep inside an empty cave where I seemed to be

207

stuck—in a world without shadows, without substance, and without light.

The last thing I remembered that night (an evening several years before I gave my life to Christ) was climbing into bed. My friends and I had been out getting high. On the weekends, we drove around cruising the hot spots. To me it was innocent fun, a time of youthful experimentation. It was the era of the Beatles and the Rolling Stones, a chance to try new things, challenge the establishment, and buck authority. After a few hours, I looked at my watch. It was ten o'clock, time to get home, not because it was late, but because I wanted to get home before my parents did. When I arrived home, as far as I could tell, everything was all right—or so I thought. My younger brother was asleep in the next room and nothing was out of place in the house. I didn't feel anything unusual, certainly nothing that would have warned me that I was being stalked by death. There was no premonition of impending doom, no sixth sense that life was about to slip out of my grasp. With nothing but sleep in mind, I climbed into bed. Darkness descended as it usually did, but this time it was different.

The next thing I remembered was sensing the pressure of a plastic tube in my throat and hearing the sound of oxygen being forced into my lungs. The bright ceiling lights of the hospital emergency room were shining through my closed eyelids. There were many voices excitedly talking all at once. How long I had been out and why, I didn't know. However, it didn't take long for me to figure out that I was in the hospital emergency room.

Once I started regaining consciousness, the attending physician removed the tube to make it easier for me to talk.

Then the questions started; first my mother, then my father and finally one of the emergency room doctors, "Paul, what happened? *Breathe*! Have you taken drugs? *Breathe*! What did you take? How much?" *Breathe*! How strange! Couldn't I breathe on my own? Something as natural as breathing had all of a sudden become an impossible task. *Breathe*! I panicked. Nurses were assigned to stay by my bedside around the clock to tell me to do what my body had for the past sixteen years been doing very well on its own, namely, breathe. Yet, even with my life at stake, I couldn't bring myself to tell them the whole truth. I was at the mercy of people who cared more for me than I cared for myself.

Only later did I finally piece together what had happened. My father had saved my life that night. He and my mother went out to a dinner, something they did once a month. This time, he felt from the moment he left the house that something was wrong. His discomfort increased as the hours passed. Finally, unable to shake it off, my father left the party and raced across town to home. Once in the house, he made his way to the front hallway where he heard a gasping sound coming from upstairs. My father bounded up the stairs faster than he had ever done before, ignoring the discomfort in his arthritic hip. The moment he stepped into the bedroom where I was sprawled on top of the bed I stopped breathing. My airway had swollen shut as a reaction to the drugs in my system. With incredible presence of mind, he called the ambulance and then began CPR. He saved my life!

Had my father not entered the house when he did, he never would have heard the sound of death rattling its saber, and my life would have been snuffed out before it had even started. It appears God had other plans.

Do you believe in destiny? I didn't, but my near-death experience forced me to rethink a lot of things I had previously believed about myself and God. It seemed that God, even when I didn't acknowledge Him, apparently had me very much in mind. Why else would He have intervened miraculously to save me from death? Something my father said especially affected me. One evening shortly after my release from the hospital, my father said to me, "Paul, your life was spared for a purpose." Those words awakened deep inside of me a sense that life really did have design and therefore meaning. Though just a teenager, one thought slowly began to take shape: There was someone or something looking out for me.

My life *was* spared for a purpose. What else explains why I didn't join the ranks of all the other young people who lost their lives to car accidents, drugs, and war? Their lives weren't spared, but mine was. Why? It had and has everything to do with the fact that God had a purpose for me, and He was willing to duel death for it! He cheated death so that I could fulfill my divinely appointed destiny. He also has a destiny for you, something so very wonderful that He is even willing to fight death for it. Now it is time for you to take your place on the front lines of your destiny and fight for it. God does.

Pinpointing your location:

Have you discovered that special purpose for which God saved you, or are you still wandering through life consoling yourself by saying, "It is enough just to be on the journey"?

Plotting your course:

Trust in the God of your destiny, and your destiny will not slip from you. Determine in your heart to fight for what God has set before you. He has! Believe and it will be yours.

Praying in your destination:

1. _______________________________________

2. _______________________________________

3. _______________________________________

Believe for the Him-possible

"Against all hope, Abraham in hope believed and so became the father of many nations . . . . Without weakening in his faith, he faced the fact that his body was as good as dead—since he was about a hundred years old—and that Sarah's womb was also dead. Yet he did not waver through unbelief regarding the promise of God, but was strengthened in his faith and gave glory to God, being fully persuaded that God had power to do what he had promised."

(Romans 4:18–21)

It is not unusual for the Lord to thrust us into positions where we must believe Him to do the *impossible* in order for us to come out of them alive and on top. Being a water-walker is all about the realms of the *Him-possible*. In fact, apparent impossibilities are the rule rather than the exception for those who wish to take the journey. More often than not, this road of growth and increase is paved with miracles.

The higher you climb and the deeper in you go, the more you discover that this ability to believe God for the impossible is, in fact, the bridge that gives us passage from lesser faith to greater faith and from lesser glory to greater glory. The truth is, you and I can't get from point A to point B in God's plan for our lives without it. Each person God uses to advance the Kingdom at one time or the other has to believe God for the miraculous. The God-kind of faith is the soil in which God-birthed ministries and God-called ministers grow best. Abraham had to learn that the God who called him did not need to turn the clock back to infuse new life into his tired body. He only needed to move the clock's hands forward, closer to the day of resurrection and restoration. He needed to learn that the God of promise was also the God of power. Sarah had to believe that the God of procreation was also the Master of the new creation.

Would Moses believe God for miraculous deliverance from a sight-enshrouded world or surrender to the murky vision of the comfortable and commercial? It was absolutely necessary for Moses to look past the wood of his staff to the will of his Lord, past the words of earthly kings and past his own failed efforts fueled by human strength to the ways of his heavenly Sovereign; past all of that to a place where he could exercise faith for a future with God rather a present without Him.

Peter found no exception to this rule. He learned that while prisons might succeed in locking some people in, they weren't capable of keeping angels out. Paul knew that while his enemies tried their best to kill him, God did His best so that he might remain alive.

Since the beginning of our journey into His presence, He has been injecting His strength into our spirits, infusing His ability into our hearts, creating the *us* of which He has always dreamed. Block by block, truth by truth, revelation by revelation, He tirelessly works. He does so precisely so that we who are equipped with His supernatural faith and courage can face and overcome any human impossibility that we find on the road of divine appointments.

If you want God to use you to do the incredible and the extraordinary, the breathtaking and the heart-stopping, then you must begin to believe for the Him-possible. This is the way it has always been and the way it will always be between God and His people in matters of renewal and resurrection while on the journey into His strength.

Pinpointing your location:

What are some of the instances in your life in which you leaned upon your own understanding more than on the Lord's?

Plotting your course:

It isn't an apparent short supply of miracles that accounts for their rarity. It is the rarity of supernatural faith that does. Where revival is, neither will be lacking.

Praying in your destination:

1. ________________________________

2. ________________________________

3. ________________________________

CONTINUING THE JOURNEY . . .

Postscript

Journeys have beginnings, but not necessarily endings. Your journey has just begun. For the past forty days you have been on a journey into His presence, learning His *ways* (the mysteries of His movements) and His *whereabouts* (how to find Him in the business of your daily life). You have been led step-by-step along a path of discovery—discovery of self and discovery of God—and most importantly a discovery of *who* and *what* God can be *in us* and who and what we can be *in Him*.

The river of revival and the winds of renewal have hopefully carried you beyond the point of no return, the point past which you find yourself so in love with Jesus and so alive in God that you would never consider moving back to safer ground or returning to more familiar territory. Pass that marker, and you are well on your way to a lifetime of indescribably beautiful experiences in God. Get past that point, and you will find that anything is possible to you. Even walking on water will be within your grasp because your faith will have finally tapped into the source of His eternally flowing strength, the source of perpetual renewal. Live each day to the fullest and enjoy your journey in the waters of His purposes and plans!

The Beginning . . . .

Biographical Sketch of the Author

Dr. Paul Allyn and his wife, Eileen, have served as missionaries to the Dominican Republic since 1980. Their daughter, Katie, was born on the field. The Allyns are the founders of *Harvest Now Ministries, Inc.* in the United States and *Ministerio El Calvario* in the Dominican Republic which serves as the organizational umbrella for their various ministries and as a ministerial covering for ministers and ministries in the Dominican Republic.

Dr. Allyn is both a minister of the Gospel and physician who has dedicated his life to making Christ known among the nations. He has been a pioneer in revival in the Dominican Republic and is committed to bringing Christ's Body into the fullness of revival and the perfection of unity.

The Allyns carry on a unique ministry of church planting, leadership training, health outreaches, revival, and renewal crusades, as well as a national conference and seminar ministry. Their ministry is also actively mobilizing Dominicans for missions, impacts churches all across the Dominican Republic. Dr. Allyn is much in demand as a special speaker and guest preacher. Through his powerful preaching ministry, he has been motivating people to enter into God's fullness for more than thirty years.

Last, but not least, Dr. Allyn has pioneered a Spanish language radio ministry that reaches into thousands of homes. Dr. Allyn has taken his passion for leadership training to the airwaves in his weekly radio program "Un Encuentro Con Los Líderes" (Leadership Encounter), through which thousands are being challenged and trained to grow into the leaders God wants them to be.

To order additional copies of

living IN THE *flow*

Have your credit card ready and call:

1-877-421-READ (7323)

or please visit our web site at
www.pleasantword.com

Also available at:
www.amazon.com
and
www.barnesandnoble.com